Spin Casting Brilliantly

Spin Casting Brilliantly

Michael Rutter and J. Alan Baumgarten

Illustrated by E. R. Jenne and Greg Siple

Mountain Press Publishing Company
Missoula, Montana
2000

Library of Congress Cataloging in Publication Data

Rutter, Michael, 1953–
    Spin casting brilliantly / Michael Rutter and J. Alan Baumgarten ;
illustrated by E. R. Jenne and Greg Siple.
        p.   cm.
Includes bibliographical references (p.   ) and index.
    ISBN 0-87842-416-4 (pbk. : alk. paper)
    1. Spin fishing.   I. Baumgarten, Alan.   II. Title.
    SH456.5 .R88 2000
    799.1'26—dc21
                                                            00-009347

PRINTED IN THE UNITED STATES OF AMERICA

Mountain Press Publishing Company
P.O. Box 2399
Missoula, Montana 59806
(406) 728-1900 • fax (406) 728-1635

We would like to thank our wives,
Shari and Sharry.

DON'T PANIC!

CONTENTS

1

INTRODUCTION
The Fine Art of Spin Casting

As no man is born an artist, so no man is born an angler.
—Izaak Walton, *The Compleat Angler*

There's a fishing postulate no one questions: *10 percent of the fishermen catch 90 percent of the fish.*

Our job is to get you into that 10 percent category. Your job is to follow our instructions and practice the techniques we suggest. We're writing this book from our fishing experience, not from some soft armchair. We know what works and what doesn't because we're on the water a hundred days a year. And when we're not fishing, we're thinking about it.

Spin fishing isn't difficult, but it's more technical than most anglers realize (which is why 10 percent catch 90 percent). With some practice, a remodeled tackle box, and this book, you too can discover the noble and uplifting pursuit of attracting fish with artificial lures. The spincasting learning curve is quick, so anyone can be intelligently catching big fish in no time. This is not to say, of course, that you'll be a master in a month. There's an undisputed level of artistry in spin casting that can take a lifetime to achieve. But we will help you develop the fundamentals so you will begin to see your tackle box as an artist's palette of lures and the water as a canvas awaiting your artful cast.

Let us take the guesswork out of where to start. We'll outline the skills every spin caster needs to know in clear, easy-to-follow chapters.

Fishing is a matter of skill, strategy, and art.

In this book you will learn

- How to select the right spinning equipment
- How to master basic spinning casts
- How to pick the right spinning tackle
- How to properly present a spinner to hungry fish
- How to read fishing water
- How to fish spinners for trout and other species

Spin casting is not for the sedentary. Leave your folding lawn chair on the back porch—the type of fishing we are going to teach you requires that both your mind and your rod be in motion. Since the fish won't come to you, you'll be going to them, thoughtfully pursuing your prey, casting and retrieving lures, setting the hook, and fighting fish. To catch fish—lots of fish, big fish—with grace and style, you must think. This is what *Spin Casting Brilliantly* is about—fishing smarter and harder.

As we said, becoming an expert spin caster isn't difficult, but it may take years to truly master all the elements. That's what makes it fun and rewarding. Fishing is, gratefully, a lifetime sport you'll never outgrow.

WE'RE ALWAYS THINKING ABOUT FISHING.

2
RODS, REELS, AND OTHER STUFF
Gearing Up to Fish

Let us say this here and now: knowledge of the fish and your ability to read water are the most important parts of this sport. Upscale gear is nice, and it does help, but it's not as important to the sport as writers, gear manufacturers, Madison Avenue ad execs, and magazine articles want you to think. It's important not to get carried away on the latest, bestest, up-to-datest gear train.

Mike's first rod was a green willow stick. He tells the story.

> My dad and I were camping on 4-Bit Crick in the Cascades of southern Oregon. After we set up camp, we wandered over to a likely clump of willow near a stand of old-growth pine. He cut a switch with his knife and carefully tied on some leader. Then, he threaded a piece of bright red yarn on a number 18 salmon egg hook.
>
> He cut me loose on the stream and I fished every pocket within a hundred yards of camp. By an undercut bank near our camp, I hooked a seven-inch rainbow, which to this day is one of the greatest trophies of my life. The creek was small, and I'm sure they didn't come much bigger in that water.
>
> I pulled my trophy in and have never been prouder—nor have I ever seen my dad prouder. He nearly burst his buttons. This was my first wild fish—and perhaps my best. I hope my son's first wild fish was just as good.

No question about it, spin casting is a gear-oriented sport. But there's something about having and wanting gear that can get out of control if you aren't careful. Though poor equipment can seriously affect your performance, you don't have to max out another gold card to get set up. In this chapter we will show you the equipment a beginner needs to start, and we'll show more advanced casters some tools that will give them an extra edge.

Michael's son Jon-Michael with fish

Michael's grandfather used to catch salmon on the Rogue River in southern Oregon with this old reel.

your current budget, the species of fish you pursue most often, the type of water you expect to fish, and how often you plan to fish. We will teach you what you need to know about

- Reels
- Rods
- Lines
- Vests
- Waders
- Clothing
- Accessories

Spin casting is a catch-all term for any sort of fishing that ain't blue-blooded fly casting, worm drowning, or worse, flinging wads of stinky, florescent PowerBait. If you're casting an artificial lure and it isn't a fly, what you're doing can likely be called spin casting.

Nowadays, the word *spin casting* or *spinning* has become rather generic—meaning any sort of fishing with an artificial lure. While it isn't fly-fishing or bait fishing, the lines occasionally get a little bit hazy when you fling a jig, Rooster Tail, or a pork ring. Let's try and clear the water with a few loose definitions.

Then we'll talk about the extras you might want to add later. If you can talk your spouse into a Range Rover and a bass boat, fine. But not everyone has the luxury of being able to get everything all at once. Frankly, there are some items you can do without. We'll help you sort through the *needs* and the *wants*.

We will present a general overview to help you determine what the best choices are for

A mess of spinning reels from the past decade. If you're not careful, you can collect a lot of gear.

BAITCASTING AND SPINNING REELS

Baitcasting Reel

The baitcasting reel is a product of Yankee ingenuity invented nearly two hundred years ago by a worm drowner named George Snyder in Kentucky. A baitcasting reel has a spool at a right angle to the rod. To cast, you press a button and the spool spins, unwinding line as you fling the bait.

Although the baitcasting reel was designed to fling bait, it didn't take long before it was in high demand for casting wooden plugs, spoons, poppers, and other artificial lures. Nowadays, a reel of this nature is still called a bait reel, even though many have never cast a piece of bait. They are excellent for spinners.

Spinning Reel

Originally *spinning* referred to the wobbling motion of a hooked minnow retrieved on a line to attract larger, predatory fish. Eventually, a clever angler fashioned an artificial lure to imitate the death throes of a baitfish. The first spinning reel as we know it was invented in the United Kingdom about a hundred years ago. A spinning reel's spool is parallel to the rod. No parts of the spool move during the cast; rather the weight of the lure and the action of the rod work to pull coils of line off the spool with little resistance. It's a rather simple, brilliant process. There have been a lot of improvements to spinning reels, but the basic concept hasn't changed.

A good reel is an investment and will last you a long time. A cheap reel is a cheap reel

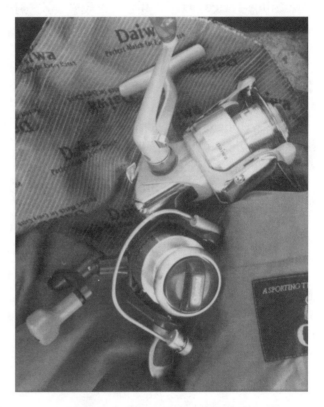

A good-quality reel like this Daiwa or this Zebco will last for years.

Baitcasting reel (left) *and spinning reel* (right)

and will let you down sooner or later. Make sure you throw it away properly, not through your windshield in a fit of anger. If you're willing to pay for quality, we have a few suggestions.

We think Zebco and Daiwa make some pretty fine reels—especially their middle- and upper-end products. These reels are a good investment. Alan is very fond of the Daiwa Regal spinning series, especially the Regal Z. (If you've got money to burn, the Emblem Z is his favorite.) He also thinks the Team Daiwa baitcasting reels, the TD-X and the higher-end X-Treme, have "good guts!"

Michael considers the Zebco Quantum E7 reel a "serious piece of fishing gear" and about the best reel for the angler's buck. For a little more money, the EM7 reel gives you the Magnum Drag System and aluminum body. All E7s have seven ball bearings that make the reel really smooth to operate. The E5 is a pretty good reel for the money (five ball bearings). The E3 is as low as he recommends. He likes the EX series for bait casting.

Shimano, Penn, and Abu Garcia all make a pretty good reel if you go with their midlevel products. We're not overly impressed with Cabela's reels (their rods are a different story). Avoid Mitchell reels—fine in the days of yore—unless you need a paperweight.

Rod Selection

Most of us grew up using anything we could get our hands on. There's nothing wrong with that. Any sort of fishing is better than no fishing at all. And if you're like Michael, you caught your first fish with a willow stick.

You can be as sophisticated or as austere with your gear as you like. One of the best fisherman we know, a man who's set a lot of records, uses an old 1960 South Bend glass rod and a thrice-rebuilt Mitchell reel (an old Mitchell, one of the good ones). He's anti-gear.

Nevertheless, there's a science to rod building, and a good rod will give you a certain

advantage. We want you to have a working knowledge of rods so you can make informed choices. Look at rods in your favorite catalog—there are pages. Take a stroll through a sporting goods store, or the sporting goods department in Kmart or Wal-mart, and you'll see forests of fishing rods nestled in a seemingly never-ending stack of rod stands. So which one is right for you? No wonder our clever fishing friend sticks with his old South Bend, letting technology march past him. Life has become too damn complicated.

In desperation, most of us just grab something that looks about right, check the price tag for sticker shock, and zip up to the check stand before the rod-jungle headache worsens. These days the tendency to specialize has created a rod for every purpose. Obviously, a specialty rod does what it was designed for well, even if it might be less than adequate for all-

Rods come in different lengths.

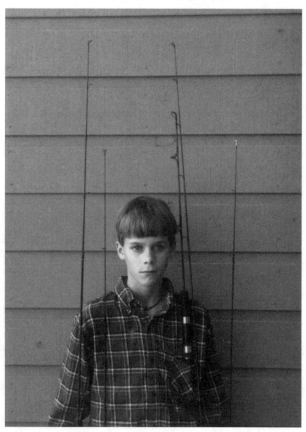

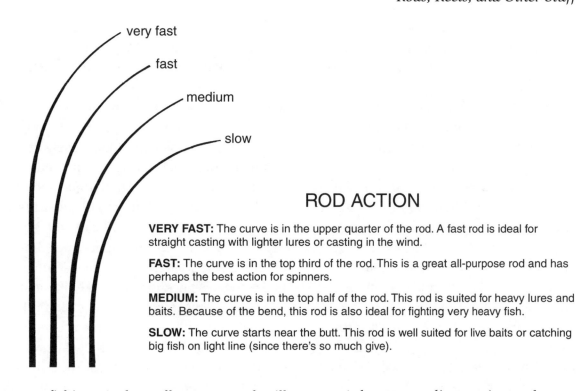

ROD ACTION

VERY FAST: The curve is in the upper quarter of the rod. A fast rod is ideal for straight casting with lighter lures or casting in the wind.

FAST: The curve is in the top third of the rod. This is a great all-purpose rod and has perhaps the best action for spinners.

MEDIUM: The curve is in the top half of the rod. This rod is suited for heavy lures and baits. Because of the bend, this rod is also ideal for fighting very heavy fish.

SLOW: The curve starts near the butt. This rod is well suited for live baits or catching big fish on light line (since there's so much give).

purpose fishing. And an all-purpose rod will do a little bit of everything but won't be as ideally suited for specialized needs. It's a trade-off. If you're very wealthy, you'll have a rod for every occasion. If you're like most of us, you'll have several rods to cover all your fishing needs. Once you determine the type of fishing you do most, you can purchase a rod that will meet most of your needs.

Actions and Lengths

Rod action refers to the point at which the rod bends when flexed. A fast-action rod bends near the tip, while a slower rod bends near the butt (the handle). Rods have extra-fast, fast, medium, and slow actions. Each of these flexes serve a different purpose for the angler. Rods also come in different lengths.

For example, a short rod with a fast action will throw a lure accurately yet is sensitive enough in the tip section that you can feel the bottom or a fish when it takes your lure. This rod will also have enough power to set the hook on a hard-mouthed bass, but it won't be overbearing on a softer-mouthed trout. A short, fast-action rod is ideal for small spinners and jigs.

A longer, medium-action rod can throw hardware with a little more weight to it. This rod's deeper bend adds power to the cast, which more effectively thrusts a heavier lure to your

Notice where this fast-action rod bends when playing a fish.

target. Also, since there's more give, you have more sweep (rod tip movement) when you set the hook and when you play the fish.

After a while, you get a feel for what you like. For most spin casters, a fast-action rod is the best choice for an all-purpose rod. A fast-action rod bends in the upper third of the rod and is very handy when playing fish or when throwing a bigger lure than the manufacturer recommends. An extra-fast action bends in the top quarter and will fling a lure well in very windy conditions, but there's not enough give and the rod is too specialized. A medium-action rod has a lot more curve and is good for large, heavy lures and plugs but not for flinging smaller tackle.

We mostly use fast-action rods. Michael likes 6- to 7-foot rods, while Alan prefers a longer rod, which has a little more give. It's a matter of taste and fishing conditions. Michael fishes in brush, where a shorter rod is advantageous. He doesn't need quite as much casting distance and likes the control a shorter rod gives him. Alan often fishes in float tubes, where a longer rod helps increase his cast, and he sometimes fishes the banks of alpine lakes, where a longer cast is more essential.

Manufacturer Recommendations on Rods

Now that you know about action and length, it's important to know what sort of fishing you'll do—and what types of lures you'll mostly throw. When you look closely at a rod you'll see that each has a recommended lure weight written on the shaft right above the handle, indicating what weight lures the rod manufacturer has designed the rod for. It might say ¼ to ⅝ ounce, ⅙ to ½ ounce, ⅜ to 1 ounce. or any dozen other combinations. You need to find a rod designed to take a lure that matches your need. This is not to say you can't fling a l-ounce lure with a rod designed for a ¹⁄₃₂- to ¼-ounce spinner. We've cast a lot of heavy lures on light rods, especially on backpacking trips in the high country; it's simply not something you'd want to do all the time since a heavier rod would be better suited for the task.

For us, a good general purpose rod should be suited to throw a ¼- to ½-ounce lure. A rod in this class can still fling a ¹⁄₁₆- or ¹⁄₃₂-ounce lure with some precision or chuck a 1-ounce plug if the occasion arises. Certainly, it stands to reason that if you are fishing on smaller waters that require precise and delicate

You can read the fine print on this rod to see how long it is and what sizes of lures and weight lines work best with it.

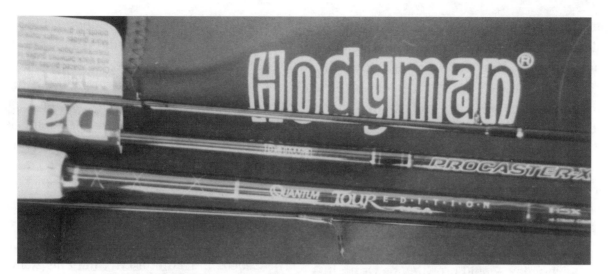

A good rod is an important part of your tackle. Important information about the rod is written above the handle.

presentations, you might want your all-purpose rod to be designed for $\frac{1}{16}$- to $\frac{1}{4}$-ounce lures. Or if you mostly fish for bass, walleye, or pike, and plugs and bigger spoons are your terminal tackle, you'll want a rod that can handle $\frac{3}{8}$- to 1-ounce lures.

In theory, your tackle should be geared to the type of fishing you are doing. But there are no real rules; do what works for you and what fits your budget. Many anglers love to catch big fish with ultralight tackle for the challenge. Folks who simply want to eat the fish they catch might use heavier gear to ensure their finned entrée makes it to the bank.

In addition to the other things we've discussed about rods, you need to consider the line it's designed to throw. Just as a rod is made to fling a specific lure weight, it's also designed for a certain pound-test line. Look on the rod near its suggested lure size and you should also see a suggested line weight or pound-test. It might read "8 to 17 line weight," "2 to 8 pound- test, "4 to 10 test," "6 to 16 line pound-test"—you get the idea.

Although line weights and line diameters vary, this designation gives you an idea about what lines are best suited for your rod. We've found the best performance comes from using a line somewhere in the middle of the recommended zone. For example, if a rod says it is suited for 2- to 8-pound-test line, it's a reasonable assumption that a 4- or 6-pound-test line will work quite handily.

By the same consideration, you won't lose a lot of performance using 4-pound-test line on a rod designed for 6- to 12-test line. Nor would it hurt much to use 14-test line on the same rod. A line slightly outside the manufacturer's specifications might alter distance to some degree, but it won't keep you from fishing. Sometimes you just have to make do.

Is a More Expensive Rod Worth the Extra Cost?

That depends on the kind of fishing that you're doing, how often you fish, where you fish, and what sort of fish you are after. You're more likely to need a sensitive, expensive rod if you're fishing lighter spinners and fishing nymphs (flies) on the bottom of the stream. You're also likely to need a sensitive rod if you're doing a lot of vertical jigging, especially in deep water. If you are pitching hardware a long way, and your pitch has to be precise and accurate, a good rod is also a must. If you're trolling Flatfish from a boat or flinging spoons at northern pike, you don't need as much rod.

Somewhere there's a practical ground where budget and needs meet. You only want to pay for bells and whistles if they will help you hook and reel in fish. We've found higher-end rods, but not top-of-the-line rods, are the best value. Nor do we need rod insert weights to "perfectly" balance the rod to our reel or have silicon carbide rings that deliver "better strength and heights." All this stuff is nice, and if you were fishing every day, would probably be worth it. But the rod in question costs about $135. For either of us, a less expensive $60 rod would do almost as well (especially when our children need braces and insist on music lessons).

You should also consider rod construction. Not all rods are made the same way. Better rods are made more carefully, are lighter, and more sensitive than low-end rods. Most rods are made of graphite. Rod manufacturers using a high-quality graphite can make a much lighter, thinner rod with a great deal of strength, precision, and reserved power that won't leave you with a sore arm at the end of the day. A really high-end rod will have 80-plus tensile modulus in a million psi. Manufacturers determine the modulus rating by counting the number of fibers in the graphite. The more modulus in a rod, the higher quality the graphite. Higher-quality fibers (modulus) are more compact and have very dense properties. Such a rod will be a great performer, but you won't have sticker shock.

Cabela's makes a very good mid- and upper-end rod. Michael has used a moderately priced Cabela's Pro Guide that performed well under a wide variety of fishing circumstances. Zebco also makes a good product, especially the Tour Edition HSX, if you have the money. The Zebco Tour Edition IM7, the Energy IM7, and the moderately priced Energy are pretty good rods. The Daiwa Procaster, the Procaster-X, and the Heartland are very good rods; Sage makes a wonderful higher-end rod (the Graphite III Series). The Sage rod is pricey but will last a lifetime.

LINES AND LINE SELECTION

If you believe the barrage of line ads, you'll need four dozen specialized lines to complement your every type of fishing. Most serious casters will have a few rods and reels with different lines to cover their needs. Each line has a purpose, but for most casters it's a bit much.

When three-year-olds go fishing together, lines will tangle. Sometimes it's easier to cut the line and start over.

The Least You Should Know about Lines

Line is calibrated or rated in pound-test, the number of pounds of pressure it takes to snap the line. For example a 5-pound-test line should break when 5 pounds of pressure are applied. There is a lot of "country latitude" among different line manufactures. Some lines actually do break at the suggested breaking point. Others have a lot more "stretch" and break considerably higher. If you are trying to set records, lines like Stren are designed to break where they say they will.

Our good friend Gary Frazier caught a nice lake trout on Fish Lake a few years ago using 4-pound-test line. With that light of line, the fish would have made the record books. However, when he had his line officially "tested," the line proved to be really 9.5-pound-test line; in other words, his 4-pound-test line didn't break until almost 10 pounds of pressure were applied. He didn't make the books, even though he nailed a darn-fine lake trout.

There is also line shock to consider. When a large fish or a snag pulls your line, your line is shocked. A cheap line will break more readily if shocked—and you don't want this to happen. At the least, shock will severely weaken a cheap line. All lines stretch, but some lines stretch more than others. A certain amount of stretch is good, because the elasticity acts like a shock absorber against a thrashing fish. However, a cheap line can drastically weaken after a single stretch. Good anglers cut a foot or two off their line every time they catch a good fish, or even every few hours, to get that stretched line off. Good line is also more resistant to abrasion than cheap line. A good, premium line doesn't weaken as much as a cheap line at the knot, the weakest link in your tackle.

For nearly all your spinning needs, you'll be using monofilament or braided line.

Monofilament Line. This is what most of us use most of the time. It's made from nylon, rather clear, strong, and flexible. It's also somewhat camouflaged when in the water, relatively abrasion resistant, and tough. Mono line will be your line of choice for nearly every fishing situation.

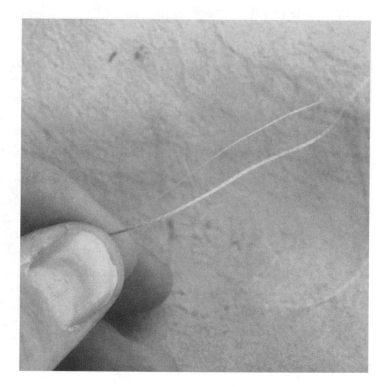

Monofilament line and braided line

Braided Lines. In the early 1990s, there was a new twist (pun intended) on lines. Mono lines were the par. However, as fishing became more specialized and sophisticated, and thanks to new miracle fibers like Kevlar, a renewed interest in braided lines surfaced. Early braided lines made from high-tech materials had a fair share of problems, including poor knot strength and the tendency to cut themselves when tied. Luckily, these problems are now history.

Braided lines are about four or five times stronger than mono lines but still have the same thickness. Knot strength is very good. This line is especially useful when fishing around a lot of structure or going deep (down rigging or deep trolling). The line is so strong you'll usually straighten your hooks before you break off. This is also useful line when dealing with larger fish in heavy structure.

We used a braided line on pike last summer in Canada. The water was choked with logjams and such. It was possible to horse the fish if you needed to, keeping it from the structure that would bust off even the best mono line. Because of the lack of stretch, the line is very sensitive. You can feel the slightest pickup and are able to set the hook an instant earlier than with monofilament.

When jigging the bottom, like we did on this trip for Canadian walleye, we had more control and could feel the action of our jig or plug as it jumped across the bottom. We could also really feel the lure's action in the water— and when something interrupted it. Setting the hook is also more sure since there's no stretch.

Braided line has a lot of pluses. We really like the sensitivity and the feel. However, except in some settings, we don't use it that often. For us, half the challenge of catching big fish is knowing that unless you do your job very well, the big fish can and will break your line. For that reason, we prefer the challenge of catching bigger fish on lighter mono line. It's pretty impossible to break off this line even

Your Old Mono Line

How do you ditch your old mono line?

Discarded mono line is an environmental hazard. Because nylon monofilament degrades very slowly, wads of old line can trap and kill birds or small animals that catch their feet in the curls. It can also catch and kill fish, if left in the water.

Don't discard your old line outside. Take it home and dump it in the trash or burn it completely. If you see wads of line that some foolish jerk has left, pick it up and know that you've helped make the world a little safer for some wild critter. We can't begin to number the dead birds we've seen trapped in old, discarded mono.

Line Hints

Below are a few tips we've learned the hard way:

1. *Always carry an extra spool for your reel.* Better yet, carry two. Some rods and reels have a wider tolerance for line sizes—a couple extra spools gives you versatility. At the least, you'll have extra line if you need it.

2. *Be careful when you put line on your reel.* If you don't fish a lot, have it done at your tackle shop for a few cents more a foot. Most shops are so experienced at doing this they could do it in their sleep. You don't want your line wound too tight or too loose. If the line is too tightly applied, it can crack the graphite spool; if it's too loose, it will loop off and cast poorly.

3. *When you reel on line, don't under- or overwind it.* This will hamper performance. Some shops tend to overwind since they get paid by the foot or yard. Don't let them! Reels have a line weight/yardage chart on them. Do not exceed this.

4. *Change your line at least once a year.* Line wears as it gets old and brittle. If you fish for big fish or have caught several big fish, change it more often. Presupposing we don't get spooled, we change our line each spring and at midsummer.

if you are the ultimate "horsing" fisherman. We recommend, though, that everyone—especially bass and walleye boys who fish the thickly structured waters—try braided line and see if it fits their needs.

Matching Things Up

As we've discussed, your rod will have a range of lines it's suited for, and so will your reel. Both of these should match. As you become more experienced, you can run a lighter line on your rig, but we can't believe the number of frustrated casters who have fallen victim to crow's nests, poor casts, and lost fish from line improperly matched to their rod.

WADERS FOR DOGS, WITH OPTIONAL TACKLE BOX RACK

VESTS, BOXES, AND SUCH TO HOLD YOUR GEAR

You'll need some place to carry your stuff. If you're in a boat, you'll need something to store your gear. If you're fishing a stream or river and you're moving very far from your camp or car, you might want a vest, a fanny pack, or big pockets to carry some tackle so you won't have to run back to the car for lures.

It's hard to recommend a great system, since we've not yet found one. For boat fishing we've tried the giant tackle box route; switched to multiple smaller tackle boxes; then changed to plastic boxes that fit in soft-sided cases. Everything has its advantages and drawbacks. We even went on an austere thing where we hit the water with a handful of lures and simply made do.

With stream spin casting you don't have to carry as many odds and ends—but it's a good idea to have a few things. Depending on the type of fishing you do, select a "carrying" system to suit your needs. Fish for a while, talk to others, and then decide what you want. Don't buy an expensive carrying system until you know.

We've tried every carrying system out there. And we're still looking.

Waders and Boots

You have to get near enough to the fish so you can cast productively. You might fish from the bank, fish from a boat or a canoe, or wade. Successful stream casters wade because it's often the best way to approach the fish without spooking them and the best way to get close enough to cast (getting free from bushes so your line on the back cast doesn't tangle up). You don't need waders if the water is warm or shallow, or if you have room to cast from the bank. But this is often hard to line up.

Chest waders come up to your chest and allow you to safely wade in waist-deep water. Hip waders are thigh high and allow you to wade in a bit over your knees. Unless you fish in really small streams, chest waders are probably the most practical.

Whether chest or hip, your waders will be either bootfoot or stockingfoot. Bootfoot waders have boots built into them. They are nice for quick fishing trips but do not have a great deal of support and aren't comfortable if you're hiking a long way. Bootfoot waders are not as secure in rough water, either. They tend to leak around the seams after a while and are hard to repair.

Stockingfoot waders have no built-in shoe/boot. You have to buy the shoe/boot separately. Most serious fisherman use these, especially those who do a fair amount of hiking to get to good water or those who wade in rougher water. If you take a look at casters on a major water, you'll find most are wearing stocking waders. They give you a lot of support and are warmer and more comfortable. We recommend you take a hard look at stockingfoot waders.

Waders come in three materials: breathable fabrics, neoprene, and rubber.

Breathable waders are one of the nicest things to come out in the last few years. Breath-

Breathable waders

Neoprene waders

"JIM, WHEN I SAID YOU WOULD NEED TO BRING WADERS, YOU MISUNDERSTOOD!"

able fabrics such as Gore-Tex allow moisture vapor to escape through pores in the fabric small enough to prevent water from coming in. On warm days you'll stay cooler, and during colder weather, with a pair of wicking long johns and fleece or wool, you can wick moisture from your body that would otherwise remain trapped against your skin and make you cold. They are like a second pair of baggy pants—not a thick and often heavy second skin—and fold up in less than half the space of neoprene or rubber waders.

Breathable waders today are typically reinforced with a sturdy fabric from the shoe to the knee—the area especially susceptible when brush busting—to help prevent a puncture or tear. The thicker the fabric the less breathable the wader, but it will be more likely to resist abuse. Still, these types of waders are the most delicate of the three, but they patch easily and, if you're careful, are a wonderful way to go. We've been very pleased with ours. They are a little pricey, but worth the money if you do a lot of wading.

We've field-tested a number of breathable waders and have found some good brands on the market. Michael has been extremely fond of Orvis's No Sweat Wader, which is moderately priced for a breathable. Soft and pliable, it's one of the most comfortable waders he's ever worn. If your fishing doesn't take you through a lot of brush, this is a dang fine wader. Orvis, by the way, doesn't make any junk. The Orvis products we've owned have lasted for years.

Hodgman also makes a very good breathable wader. It's a little heavier than the Orvis, and a little tougher if you're doing any brush busting—but not quite as breathable as the Orvis. Both are reasonably priced and a good product. Mike is a big fan of breathables; Alan isn't.

Neoprene waders are popular with many casters because there is a minimal amount of current drag, since they fit snugly. While they're more expensive than rubber waders, they last a lot longer and don't crack. If they do need repairs, they are easy to fix. You can buy different

Alan, decked out in neoprene, is admiring a fine winter brown.

neoprene weights depending on how late in the season you fish and how cold the water is.

Alan is a big fan of Hodgman neoprenes and boots, as you'll see in some of these photos. He owns three pairs in different thicknesses for varying water and weather conditions. He's withholding judgment on breathable waders until the manufacturers do a little more R&D.

Rubber waders can be purchased very cheaply and will last a season or two. Or you can spend about double the price and get a good set. There is more drag when you are in the current or kicking in a float tube, but rubber waders, even a cheaper set, will serve you. Plan on replacing rubber waders about once a year, an expensive pair maybe every two years. No matter how well you take care of them, they weather and crack.

Lastly, especially with rubber waders, wear an outside belt so if you fall, your waders won't fill up with water. If you have a belt on, you'll get wet, but the air pocket from your feet to your waist will help you float.

CLOTHING

Everyone has an opinion on clothes, and so do we. We can't speak for others, but ours is founded in experience (roughly translated, learning the hard way). L. L. Bean, Cabela's, and Orvis all offer a good selection of gear. L. L. Bean and Orvis have good products; it's hard to go wrong with their stuff. Cabela's has a wider range of quality, so we'd suggest looking at the mid- to upper-range items. Each of these mail-order houses stands behind everything it sells and is excellent to work with.

When you buy clothing, think in terms of layers. If you're summer fishing, or fishing near the car, typical outdoor clothes will do. If you're pushing the weather, however, take care. The world is a friendly place, but people die out

A well-dressed fisherman always wears a vest and carries a net. When it's cold, wear more layers than you think you need.

there. Remember you are near water and there's always the possibility of getting wet.

When the weather turns cool, remember that cotton, while great for warm weather, has no insulating value when wet and will chill you fast. Down also is a killer when wet. Unless you're in a boat and have a backup coat, avoid down when fishing. If you like the down feel, you can use a synthetic such as Micro-loft. It's as warm as down, a little thinner, and the fibers won't absorb water, keeping you warm even when wet.

While wool has been the standard for outdoor clothes for hundreds of years, it's heavy, heavier when wet, and uncomfortable for some. We can't say enough about the fleeces that are out. They shed water, have great insulating

value, and dry fast (something that neither cotton nor down does well). If your fleece doesn't have a wind block built in, you'll need a good shell. We use Helly Hansen Deep Water Rain Parkas. This parka is waterproof but breathable, making it a great wind jacket and raincoat. When the weather is really cold, one or two pairs of poly long johns under fleece pants will keep you warm. Adjust your layering system to suit your comfort level and the conditions in which you fish.

Socks and Warm Feet

From more years on the water than we care to remember (including Michael's guiding adventures), we've seen cold feet ruin some good fishing trips. No matter how good the fishing is, when your feet are cold, it's no damn fun.

No one claims you'll ever be truly comfortable outdoors. It's always too hot or too cold. However, there are a number of things you can do to keep your feet warm (and cooler, too). Begin with a good sock system. You need a thin polyester or silk liner to wick moisture, covered by a heavier wool sock. This might sound like a lot for the summer time, but it actually keeps your feet cooler than a single sock.

We've tried a lot of socks, but for our money, Vasque's Summit Thermal is the best sock in the world.

We don't want to give you the impression that fishing is always an arctic sport, but it is important to be properly dressed for all weather conditions. When we're fishing in the sun and heat, we tend to keep covered with light, highly breathable clothing head to foot. Hours of direct sunlight can really zap your energy. On the other hand, stripping down to the ol' Speedo can have its rewards at times. You be the judge.

In any case, remember that outdoor clothing is a little more specialized and costs a little more than going-to-the-office duds. The advantage is that your gear, properly cared for, will last a long time and the first time you really need it, cost won't matter.

Accessories

Here are a few odds and ends you might want to collect later that will make your fishing easier, if not more comfortable. These items are not listed in any order of importance.

- Polarized sunglasses. Protect your eyes from sun glare and reflection while improving your view of fish activity.

- Thermometer. To see if the water is the optimum temperature.

- Net. To land your fish more easily.

- Bug dope. To keep the pests at bay (don't get any on your lures).

- Small field glasses. To look for fish activity or wildlife. Bushnell makes many varieties that fit every budget.

- Counter Assault bear spray: To feel secure in bear country. (This stuff really works, so don't get it in your eyes!) Counter Assault is the only brand we have faith in—we've used it first-hand and we're still here.

- Victorinox Swiss Army knife: To use thirty-four times a day. The SwissChamp or Fisherman are excellent choices. You can do most anything with them from gutting a fish, to fixing a reel, to clipping Rooster Tails or line with the scissors. It's the ultimate fishing tool.

- Sunscreen. To keep those UV rays off your hide and cancer at bay.

- Lunch. To eat so you don't have to waste fishing time coming in. Also, remember to bring plenty of water.

3

THE LORE OF THE LURE
Spin Casting's Underwater Hardware Connection

When you spin cast, hardware and lures—often called terminal tackle—can be broken down into three basic categories: spinners, spoons, and plugs. Let's take a moment and discuss each in turn so you'll be better able to make an educated tackle choice when fishing.

SPINNING WITH SPINNERS

As the name implies, spinners spin around when you pull them through the water, causing "good vibrations" that often induce a fish to strike—even if the fish hasn't yet focused in on the prey. Couple this with the visual flashes

There's a wide selection of lures out there, but only a few have permanent homes in our tackle boxes.

and colors of the lure, and a spinner appears to be a vulnerable baitfish.

Even when a fish isn't hungry or when the fish's feeding urge is turned off, some instinct still drives it to investigate and sometimes gobble a cleverly worked spinner. We can't count the number of spawning fish (a time when they are not supposed to eat) we've caught on spinners. We can't ask the fish why it will take a lure when it's not hungry, but we're glad it does.

Let's take a look at the two main types of spinners: in-line spinners and spinnerbaits.

In-line Spinners

Most spinners are what we call in-line spinners. As the name implies, the blades and dressing are in a line. The blade of the spinner is mounted on a straight wire shaft. Most blades are attached to the wire shaft one of three ways:

1) The blade is mounted on a U-shaped bar (a clevis), which is attached to the shaft. An example of the U-shaped blade is an Original Mepps or a Rooster Tail. The blade spins rapidly, giving a smooth, subtle vibration.

2) The blade has a hole in it and is mounted directly to the wire shaft. A Panther Martin is a good example of a "hole-in-the-blade" spinner. This type of blade produces the most vibration in the water.

3) The blade is attached to the wire shaft by a swivel (this method isn't as popular as it used to be). An example of a swivel blade is a

SPINNERS

In-line Spinners

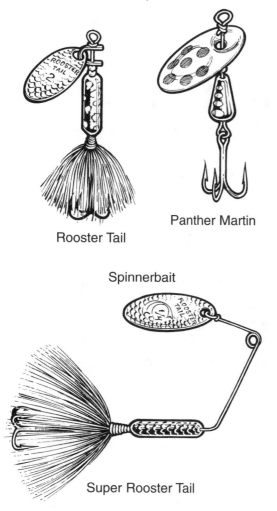

Rooster Tail

Panther Martin

Spinnerbait

Super Rooster Tail

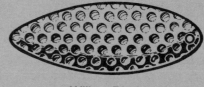

Colorado spinner. This blade wobbles, rather than spins, in the water, producing a flash.

The blade spins around the shaft or wire when pressure is applied, either by the current or when retrieving. Different blade shapes, different blade thicknesses, different attachment styles affect the action of the blade(s) in the water—all for different angling purposes.

In-line lures seem to be more popular among trout anglers than with the bass folk. Nevertheless, these types of spinners are deadly on all varieties of warm-water fish. We can't think of a fish that this type of spinner hasn't caught.

Spinnerbaits

A spinnerbait is favored more for warm-water angling, especially bass. Nevertheless, a spinnerbait is a good trout lure if you reduce the size. A spinnerbait looks like a big safety pin with a blade on one prong and a hook and dressing on the other. In the water, the blade rides on top. Blades like this come in a number of sizes. (Alan is a great fan of spinnerbaits and claims to outfish Michael nearly two-to-one when the fish are neutral. Michael remains stubbornly indifferent.)

SPINNING WITH SPOONS

Spoons have a rich and deserving history in the fishing world. They are responsible for a great number of the fish caught, and they were the most popular piece of hardware on the market until recently eclipsed by spinners.

SPOONS

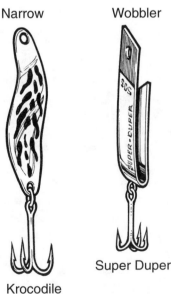

Narrow — Krocodile

Wobbler — Super Duper

Spoonlike — Dardevle

We can't begin to wonder how we would have survived pike and muskie trips to Canada, trips to the deep water for lake trout, endless days on rivers and the ocean for salmon without spoons. And on those bass fishing days

when nothing else worked, we could always count on a spoon to bring home the fish. A spoon is a great lure, one that no tackle box should be without; it is truly a universal piece of hardware with universal application.

Let's take a look at the three main types of spoons: spoonlike spoons, wobbler spoons, and narrow spoons.

"Spoonlike" Spoons

As the name suggests, this lure looks like someone has taken a kitchen spoon, ground off the handle, and drilled a hole in the end. In fact, the first spoons were likely made this way.

It is rather wide in the body. Sometimes, too, the metal is thickest in the widest portion of the lure. The action looks a lot like a very sick or wounded baitfish "wobbling" laterally about in the water. When you put pressure on

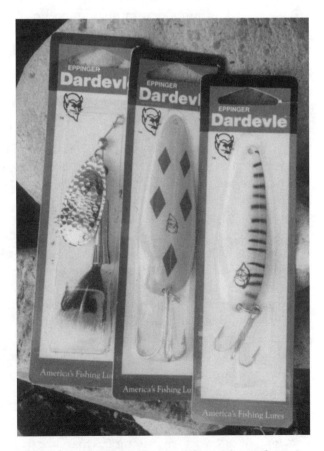

The Dardevle is an old standby and our favorite spoon. We've nailed about every species of fish on this old favorite.

the spoon, it will move laterally to a greater degree. The traditional Dardevle and the Little Cleo are very traditional lures of this nature.

Spoonlike spoons are a superior lure for aggressive fish. These fish will hit them with a passion. When fish turn neutral or finicky, however, this lure might be a little too much, scaring the fish instead of attracting them.

Wobbler Spoons

Wobbler spoons look less like a spoon and more like a strangely bent piece of metal. However, they are deadly on fish. Wobblers frequently don't have the radical action in the water that a spoonlike spoon has. They have a more subtle action and they move in the water gracefully. They will still attract a more aggressive fish—although not with the determination of a true spoon—but such lures aren't as likely to frighten a neutral fish. In fact, they often trigger a strike from a neutral fish when nothing else will. Several good examples of this lure are the Super Duper (Michael's favorite lure), the Z-Ray, and the Kastmaster.

Narrow Spoons

These spoons are somewhat spoonlike, but they are longer and more narrow. Because they have a slimmer profile, they flutter about the water. Many lures of this nature have a bent middle, imparting a great motion in the water. Like the wobblers, they are more subtle in the water. They will attract an aggressive fish, but they will also be less likely to frighten a neutral fish since there is very little lateral wobble. Our two favorite narrow spoons are the Krocodile and the Syclops.

SPINNING WITH PLUGS

Plugs are a great way to catch fish. They are used most heavily by bass casters and are heavensent for trolling. A lot of careful high-

---

Spoons: A Universal Lure

A long time ago, someone got the bright idea that a spoon would make a terrific lure. We like to think a guy in a boat was eating chili and drinking root beer and dropped his spoon overboard. As it wobbled to the bottom, the silvery flash did look a little like a fish and was consumed in the maw of a giant fish. The rest was history. Kids who couldn't afford lures were borrowing from mom's kitchen, grinding off the handle, making some modifications, and bringing in big fish.

With a little experimentation, angling inventors were sanding the edges thinner and keeping the middle a bit thicker so there would be an erratic flutter as the lure moved in the water. In 1912 the forerunner of all modern spoons, the Dardevle, was made. Before the Great Depression, a fellow named Louis Johnson perfected the configuration (thick middle and thin edges) so it would dance back and forth when retrieved.

A spoon is universal. It can be fished fast or slow, deep or shallow. It can be trolled, jigged, fluttered, retrieved, or any combination of the above. It can be a half inch or ten inches. A small ⅛-ounce spoon can be used on smaller fish, or a 4-ounce spoon can entice a big laker, muskie, or salmon.

Each spoon has a slightly different action in the water and a different purpose. We all have our favorites. Besides the Dardevle, which has caught every species known to man, there are a few others worth mentioning. There are the Acme Kastmaster, an excellent lure and great for getting deep; the Luhr Jensen Crippled Herring, one of Alan's favorites for lake trout; the Westport Wobbler; and the Hildebrandt Solo Spoon, among others.

tech design goes into plugs nowadays. It's big business, especially in the bass fishing world.

Plugs may be high-tech, but they've been around for some time. In the old days they were hand carved and carefully crafted by fish-loving artisans. Most weighed at least an ounce, so they weren't too subtle in the water. The weight was necessary to help cast the heavy rods and thick lines of yore.

Today you can choose from a dizzying array of plugs in legions of different shapes and colors. Plugs can be divided into three types: crankbait plugs, minnow plugs, and tube-shaped (or banana-shaped) plugs.

PLUGS

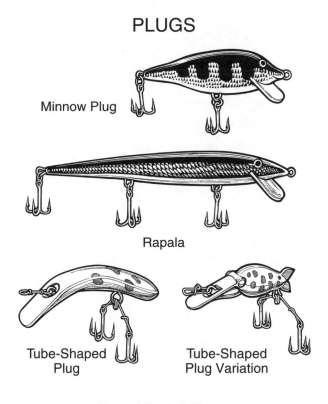

Minnow Plug

Rapala

Tube-Shaped Plug

Tube-Shaped Plug Variation

Crankbait Plugs

If there was ever a darling of the bass fishermen, it would be their trusty crankbait. Probably no other lure has more research and development behind it.

A crankbait looks sort of like a short, fat chub with a plastic Donald Duck bill. It comes in a myriad of colors and shapes. Some rattle underwater to attract fish. And depending on the size of the bill, some lures count down.

When you troll with them, reel them in, or the current puts pressure on them, you can determine, somewhat, the depth to which they dive.

They cast quite well. However, the real advantage is you can tailor your fishing to the fish. A crankbait lets you work your lure where you think the fish are. If you want a just-below-the-surface lure, you can tie on a plug for that purpose. If you want to get down ten feet, you can get a plug for that. If you want twenty or thirty feet, no problem.

While crankbaits are thought of by many as a warm-water lure, primarily for largemouth bass, they are deadly on other types of fish. We've taken more than our fair share of trout with crankbaits. When the fish were sitting neutral just off a shelf at Klamath Lake in southern Oregon, we used crankbaits to get down to their level. Nothing else worked.

A crankbait is standard fare in our lake box. They also work well on bigger rivers. And for pike when they shut down, wow! Don't leave home without them.

Michael's father used this old wooden plug when he was a boy in the Great Lakes region.

Minnow Plugs

A minnow plug might look like any of the many kinds of fish that larger fish feed on. Other lures don't always look like fish per se, even if they act or vibrate like one in the water. This type of plug makes good sense. A minnow plug might be shaped like a small brown or rainbow trout or a young bass. They are often made of plastic, but some are still made of wood. Some minnow plugs are meant to fish right under the surface (floating plugs), while others are meant to be worked deeper (sinking plugs).

Tube-Shaped (Banana-Shaped) Plugs

Where we're from in the West, we call these lures tubes, but farther east, some anglers refer to them as banana plugs since they resemble a banana with hooks. Whatever you want to call 'em, they catch fish. Every tackle box needs a few tube plugs.

If you're very old, this is the sort of plug you might have grown up using. The trusty old Flatfish, marketed by Wordens, which has been around since long before we were born, is a perfect example. This old-fashioned lure really shines when trolling—especially at slow speed. It has a distinct wobble in the water that attracts fish. We've had one-hundred-fish days on a pair of black-and-orange and frog F-4 Flatfish. You can cast a tube lure, but they aren't designed to fling like a crankbait, a spoon, or a minnow. For casting small lures, you might have to add some weight.

Besides the Flatfish, the Kwikfish and the Fire Plug are proven fish catchers. Both of these plugs are excellent when fished slowly. In this same family of plugs, but with some differences, there are the Luhr Jensen Hot Shot (a plug Michael has caught a lot of steelhead on) and the Lazy Ike. Besides being good trolling lures, these types of plugs are also very good for downstream fishing.

FISHING YOUR SPINNER, SPOON, OR PLUG

Take a few minutes and think about life under the film. If you want to catch fish, learn how a fish reacts. If a spinner is simulating a baitfish, how does it act in the water?

Watch a minnow. When was the last time you saw one swimming in a straight line for

THE LARGEST LURE EVER DEPLOYED WAS THAT USED BY CAPTAIN AHAB IN HIS QUEST FOR MOBY DICK.

fifty to one hundred feet? Our guess is you never have—it isn't baitfish-like behavior to swim straight and predictably. A small fish scrambles about the water like a running back in enemy territory. If you're a wounded minnow, you're going to flutter more, be more irregular in your movements.

Take a few minutes to watch how your lure looks in the water and work it carefully. In pressured areas, fish see a lot of lures pulled through the water. Your retrieve has everything to do with how many fish you catch. Work the lure in the water and make it alive. Stop the action of the lure, let it sink, bring it up sharply, move it from side to side, bring it in fast, bring it in slow. Bring it to life.

Buy a high-quality steel-bearing swivel and you'll get the maximum effect out of your hardware. However, when you want to work a spoon laterally in the water to full effect, tie the line directly to the split ring (which comes on the lure when you buy it) and save the swivel for another day. If your lure doesn't come with a split ring, add one. It will help your lure swing from side to side. This is especially helpful if you are trolling.

JIGS

Leave the debate about whether spinners and jigs belong in the same discussions to others. We're going to talk about them here.

Basically, a jig is a weighted head (usually lead) on a hook. Below the head, there is some sort of dressing, fashioned from a wide array of materials, that flutters as the lure is pulled through the water. There's a lot of mix and matching with jigs, and most anglers assemble their own with different combinations to meet the needs of the water that day.

Every box should have at least a small collection of jigs. You should have a few in various head sizes ($1/8$ to $1/2$ ounce). We'd also recommend you have jigs dressed with feathers and

What's in the Color of a Lure?

This is a big debate among casters that isn't likely to end soon. You'll find experts firmly entrenched on either side of this issue.

What's in a color? Maybe not much if the fish is hungry or isn't feeling selective at the moment. Some feel—and we're in this camp—that color usually isn't as important as the presentation, shape, and action of a lure. Nevertheless, there's something to color. It seems that at times the right color can give you an edge you wouldn't have had otherwise. For us, it's not worth carrying our favorite lures in every different color just to meet the whims of a selective fish.

Michael's friend, master guide Steve Partridge, disagrees with us. Steve feels that color is a critical element in fishing success and an important part of what he calls his fishing formula. Steve goes to great lengths to use the right colors. And he carries a lot of tackle as a result. Still, we can't argue with the number of fish Steve catches. He's about the best fisherman we know anywhere—on either side of the Atlantic.

Here are some rules of thumb—given as guidelines, not gospel. If you want fish to see your hardware on a bright day or in clear water, use a silver lure. On a cloudy day, or if the water is stained, use bronze (gold or copper) since fish can see it better. On cloudy days, also consider these colors: white, red, chartreuse, black, and green.

deer hair—and a variety of rubber or plastic skirts. Have a selection in different colors.

We'll discuss jigging techniques in greater detail later, but for now, you should know that jigs are wonderful for "vertical jigging," where you fish straight down and dance the jig about. You can also work jigs like a spinner, retrieving them and dancing them about in the water by moving your rod tip. You can use a jig to approximate a fish, a grub, leech, a snake, a frog, a crustacean—or simply something that looks edible and yummy.

When you jig, a selection of sizes is important. If the fish seem to ignore your offering, scale down a size or two. When dealing with aggressive fish, we've had six-inch fry attack 1-ounce jigs. An aggressive fish will take on King Kong if it can get its mouth around it. Size doesn't matter to hungry fish. If the fish are selective or passive, the key is to scale down and dance the jig more delicately. We don't know how many times we've come up zeroes on a ¼-ounce jig. We've tied them on a ⅛-ounce jig, same color and shape, same action, and have had fish line up to nail our jig.

Use plastic jigs, especially with twister and crayfish tails, for selective and passive fish. They attract the fish's attention, but they don't seem to spook them with their action unless you radically jerk them. Consider jigs when dealing with passive fish. For example, when pike shut down, they don't want to take anything; they seem to sense metal. A soft jig is about the best thing you can use. Pouting lake trout are no exception.

Realistic feel is another advantage. When a fish sinks its jaws on a plastic body, it's not as likely to spit the lure. The jig feels lifelike and alive. This gives you a little extra time to set the hook. Also, when fish are selective, they sometimes nose or bump a lure. If that lure is metal, you have a spooked fish. If the fish bumps into something soft, you aren't as prone to scare the fish, and it might hit it next with its mouth.

ALLURING LURES TO CALL YOUR OWN

It's impossible to cover every lure that will work because every situation might require different hardware. But, we've had a chance to fish with most lures on the market at one time or another and feel qualified to make a few observations on what a well-stocked vest or tackle box would consist of. Some lures seem to have a universal application—you can catch all sorts of game fish with them—even though they also have a specialized function. We suggest a good selection. However, if you are fishing mostly smaller streams, you'll want less weight and a smaller lure. If you're fishing on big rivers and lakes, go heavier. If all you're after is trout, your box will be a little different from the person who's only after bass.

Jigs should be in every angler's tackle box— they are universal lures.

Some of Our Favorite Lures

Here are some lures we think you might want to consider (not necessarily listed in order of importance). You'll also note that many of our favorites are standby lures that have been around for many years (not often the newest trendy types). There is a reason for this. They are proven favorites and have caught a lot of fish. Sometimes all the fancy stuff is designed to catch more anglers in the tackle store than fish.

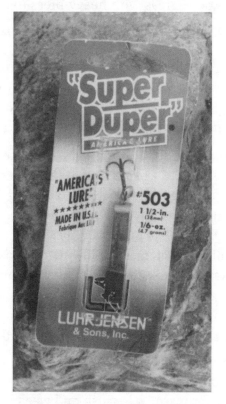

A Super Duper #503 fished right will trigger neutral fish to strike and will excite aggressive fish.

- **Super Duper #503,** ⅙ ounce (marketed by Luhr Jensen). This is Michael's lure of choice. The Super Duper has a twisting erratic action that attracts aggressive fish but doesn't spook neutral fish. In addition to all sorts of trout and panfish, Michael has nailed a thirty-five-pound lake trout, a fifteen-pound

steelhead, and a twenty-pound pike on this lure. This lure comes in a number of sizes and colors; however, the ⅙-ounce Red Head nickel and brass are our two favorites.

- **Jake's Spin-a-Lure** is one of the best lures ever made—and one of our very favorites! We can't think of a fish it won't catch. Trout, pike, and bass seem to die for this lure. Alan has used it with great success on salmon in British Columbia, and Michael has been known to use it on steelhead in southern Oregon waters. This lure, however, is deadly on cutthroat trout—if not the best lure we've ever found. In fact, one time in Yellowstone National Park, a place known for its cutts, this lure was selling for $7 a pop on the shore of the lake. Always have a handful of these lures about.

This male brown was quick to take a Jake's Spin-a-Lure . . . after ignoring every other piece of hardware we had to offer.

Don't overlook **Jake's Li'l Jakes** and the **Jake's Wobbler.** Both are excellent lures. The Li'l Wobbler is very close to the Super Duper #503 but perhaps a little tougher

- **Mepps Original Plain Aglia,** ¹⁄₁₂ to ½ ounce. This is a time-proven trout lure with excellent action. However, we can't count the number of pike and bass we've nailed on this lure (we tried to keep count one memorable hot afternoon on our favorite bass pond, but we lost track somewhere around 130). This lure is also great for steelhead. Although we tend to favor the basic silver, bronze, and red-white, any color is a good choice.

- **Panther Martin,** $1/32$ to $1/4$ ounce. A must-have stream and river lure (not bad for lakes either) that has been around for almost forty years. We've caught hundreds and hundreds and hundreds of fish on this lure. Because of the way it's constructed, the Panther vibrates in a way that seems to naturally draw fish. It comes in many colors, but black, white, gold, and silver are our favorites.

Panther Martins are a must for every tackle box.

- **Original Rooster Tail,** $1/24$ to $1/4$ ounce. Pick a color and be happy. Yellow and green are Alan's favorites; white and black are Michael's. A blade-and-feather action is a wonderful combination and a fish catcher. Don't expect these types of lures to last a long time. They get thrashed fairly fast and need frequent replacement. Rooster Tail is a

brand name, but other manufacturers like Blue Fox, Panther Martin, and Mepps make a blade-and-feather-combination lure as well. We slightly favor the Original Rooster in traditional colors—maybe out of nostalgia—but all are very good brands.

- **Mepps Black Fury,** $1/12$ to $1/2$ ounce. This is a blade with a fur tail. The Black Fury is great for selective fish or fish feeding on the surface—especially if you need a smaller lure. The black blade with yellow dots will attract a fish, but it's not too bold because the blades twirl close to the body. We use it on bright days or in areas with heavy pressure.

- We are also very fond of the **Blue Fox Foxtail,** $7/64$ to $3/8$ ounce. This lure is available in very small sizes, a real plus in delicate fishing situations or small streams. Alan fishes this lure a lot! He's had success with silver-white, silver-yellow, and hot pepper.

- **Mepps Thunder Bug,** $1/8$ to $1/4$ ounce. This looks and acts like a bug in the water. This lure can help you match a hatch. It has a segmented mayfly body, and the veined blade wings look like a Dobson fly. It comes in a number of colors, stone fly–black and white miller–white blades are our favorites. You can also get this lure without a tail. This is a great warm-water lure and a killer on trout. Consider it a must for your summer fishing needs!

- **Mepps Weedless** lures in varying sizes are great for warm-water fish and weedy conditions. This lure has a thin, flexible guard over the hook that keeps it from hanging on plants and debris but snaps out of the way when a lunker fish hits it. With a Mepps Weedless you will invariably spend more time fishing and less time breaking off your line.

- **Flatfish,** a good selection of F-4s, a few F-7s (and X-4 for bigger fish on bigger waters). This is a great lure and a must if you're trolling or fishing a river from a drift boat. Fish this lure slow and easy to bring out its wonderful action.

- **Z-Ray**, by Whitman. This wobbler has a wonderful action in the water. It's also a great lure for working near the surface. We've caught piglet-sized bass and yardstick muskie on this lure. It's also a great lure for rainbow trout on Klamath and cutthroat trout on Yellowstone Lake. Michael swears by this lure. He likes silver and brass, while Alan is partial to other colors.

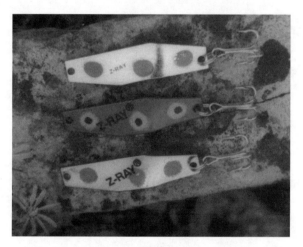

The Z-Ray's action is excellent.

- **Krocodile**, by Luhr Jensen. A fantastic lure that works well in most fishing situations. Alan likes it better than he does the Z-Ray (it has a little different action in the water). We both think this is a must for the tackle box.

- **Dardevle**. The greatest spoon of all. Red-white and yellow have been really good for us. This lure has a wonderful action. We always carry a lot of them if we're going to Canada or fishing for big trout or bass.

- **Jigs.** You need a variety of sizes and colors. We carry $1/32$- to $1/2$-ounce jigs in our boxes as a rule. We are more partial to marabou than bucktail for the dressing. We keep a selection of sizes, so we can keep selective and passive fish interested. In feathered jigs, we have black, white, green, brown, and yellow with round heads. We often tie our own with a fuller body. We keep a selection of heads in various sizes, weights, and colors, with a variety of tails to match. We use solid-color and peppered bodies. Our favorite colors are green, chartreuse, black, white, clear, pink, and red. Mike favors squid tubes; Alan, twister tails.

SAMURAI CASTER

4
GETTING THE RIGHT CAST
Let That Metal Fly

Maybe casting a spinner like a pro looks hard, but it isn't complicated. If you can move your arm enough to swat a fly, wave "bye-bye" to your significant other, or command your pit bull to devour an intruder, you can cast. Even a young child can master the basics with only a little practice. Casting accurately in actual fishing situations (brush, trees, currents, rocks, etc.), however, requires a little more practice.

For Alan, casting is a matter of concentration and mental calculation; his mind is a whirl of ballistics and mathematical formulas that would give an eighth-grade math student nightmares. For Michael, casting transcends science.

It's metaphysical. Michael doesn't think; he just lets it happen. He is at one with his cast.

Whatever your state of mind, the important thing is the result, and the only way to get results is through a lot of casting practice.

CASTING ESSENTIALS

Many casters make the understandable mistake of treating a fishing rod like an inflexible length of galvanized pipe. Not so, as you'll discover the first time your fishing buddy walks his rod tip into the back of your head. It bends

Casting is easy enough, but it takes practice to master.

alright. The flex in the rod serves two purposes. It acts as a buffer against the action of a hooked fish to keep your line from snapping. The flex in the rod is also designed to help you cast, but only if you use it the way it was intended. A caster who knows how to use the flex in his or her rod can easily send a lure double or triple the distance of an inexperienced caster. It has nothing to do with arm strength. It's just a matter of momentum.

When you cast, the forward motion bends the rod slightly—the faster you move it forward, the more bend you'll create in your rod. When you reach about 2:00, bring your rod to an abrupt stop. The tip of the rod, in a big hurry to catch up with its lower half, is now traveling forward much faster than your arm could ever make it go. Of course, your lure is following right behind it.

Release the line just as the lure flies past the rod tip. The rod will stop, but the lure will fly on in a low arc toward its goal.

Some Basic Casts You Need To Know

There are four kinds of casts you should know.

- *The basic overhead cast* is often the first cast most anglers learn and the one we use most of the time. The rod tip is nearly straight up (12:00) at the peak of the casting arc. This cast achieves the maximum distance and is for many casters their most accurate cast.

- *The low cast* is useful when you want to get your lure under overhanging bushes when stream fishing. It takes practice to be accurate with this cast, and most anglers will never get a lot of distance with it. Hunch down below the level of the brush. Holding the rod parallel to the water and about a foot above the water's surface, flick the rod to lob the lure to the strike zone.

- *The side cast* is excellent for avoiding overhanging branches or if you want side

distance. With your arm held around the 3:00 position and at waist height, cast parallel to the water. Because you hold the rod at waist height, the side cast delivers your lure much farther than the low cast does.

- *The wind cast* is a modified side cast and useful for reducing the hassles of casting in a strong wind. If you are nearly six feet and your rod is eight feet, the tip of your rod (and lure) may be from eleven to thirteen feet above the water. On a windy day, the higher you go, the more wind resistance you'll encounter. You want to lower your rod to where the wind is less of a factor. Start in the 3:00 position and swing the rod tip up to about 2:00 before you release the lure. The wind cast sends your lure out in an area that is lower than in the basic cast.

To improve the precision of any cast, practice stopping your lure in midair by reeling in one or two turns. By experimenting stopping at different points you can correct an overshot cast. You'll be glad you've worked on this technique if you fish small streams with willow- and alder-choked banks.

BACKYARD CASTING

The basics of casting may seem obvious, but experienced casters are always willing to learn something new. You should practice every day—that's what Alan's piano teacher always said, and we have no reason to think that it doesn't apply to fishing. Come to think of it, every true principle applies to fishing.

Honestly, you can be a pretty lame to average caster and still catch some good fish. You don't need the same level of precision for spin casting as you do for fly-fishing. Nevertheless, a good, precise cast could mean the difference between fishing success and a nice day outdoors. This is especially true if you are a river or stream caster. You'll want to work pockets

BASIC OVERHEAD CAST

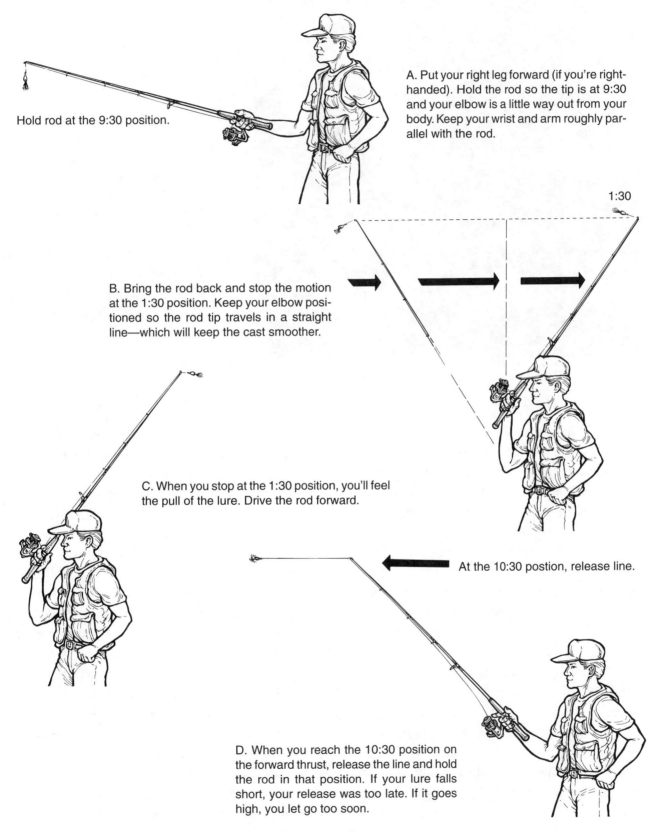

Hold rod at the 9:30 position.

A. Put your right leg forward (if you're right-handed). Hold the rod so the tip is at 9:30 and your elbow is a little way out from your body. Keep your wrist and arm roughly parallel with the rod.

1:30

B. Bring the rod back and stop the motion at the 1:30 position. Keep your elbow positioned so the rod tip travels in a straight line—which will keep the cast smoother.

C. When you stop at the 1:30 position, you'll feel the pull of the lure. Drive the rod forward.

At the 10:30 postion, release line.

D. When you reach the 10:30 position on the forward thrust, release the line and hold the rod in that position. If your lure falls short, your release was too late. If it goes high, you let go too soon.

*Precise casting
means you can fish
the most productive
water accurately and
successfully.*

or pools that require a pretty accurate cast. If you know the fish are holding in a small pocket, you have to place your lure inside a narrow casting window. If you fish lakes, unless you are working the shoreline with overhanging branches, a precise cast isn't quite as critical.

We recommend practicing in your backyard, the park, a ballfield, or any other place with adequate casting space. To practice, take the hooks off an old spinner—a spoon works well. First start with a heavy spoon, and as you gain more control, work with something lighter. This will help you get what Alan calls "the feel," or how much fling it takes to launch different-size lures (and different rods if you use several).

We've found the best way to practice is to take a few empty two-liter Coke bottles and set them up on the lawn in different places—vary your distance between ten and seventy feet—and cast to them. Your goal is to hit the bottle. After you can hit consistently, make the game more challenging.

Set up a bottle a few feet from the fence. Cast to it. The fence represents bushes and you'll get hung up if you hit it. Make life a little more interesting: move the bottle a foot from the fence. At first, cast close to your target. Then as you get good, start backing up.

Now set up a bottle under an overhanging tree or shrub. Cast to it so you don't get tangled up. Start close and work back. You'll obviously have to use a side cast. This is excellent practice. Alan became an excellent caster by casting toward a two-liter Coke bottle placed under his new Ford Explorer. His will to avoid blemishing that perfect new exterior forced him into a state of intense mental concentration, and he never missed his target. Please don't attempt this with a Chevy.

After you feel like you've got this wired, work your casts on your knees, sitting down, bending down, and from the sides. This will help you a lot. You don't always have the luxury of casting in a perfect position when you're on the water.

5
READING THE WATER
The Aquatic Library

Good casters know they can't just fling lures into any stretch of pretty water and expect to pound fish.

If you want to put the odds in your favor and see your trusty rod bend under the weight of many fish, *you have to know the water you're fishing on.* More specifically, you have to know what's going on *underneath* the surface.

You can have the finest set of clothes from L. L. Bean, Cabela's, or Dunn's. You can have a custom $600 spinning rod and a $500 spinning reel with more ball bearings than a formula race car. You can have space-age line as thin, light, and excessive as spun gold. You can have the best collection of lures in every color and size. For that matter, you can be on the finest stream or lake in the United States, Canada, New Zealand, Siberia, or Chile. It won't matter.

If you don't know where to fish, all you're going to get is expensive casting practice—albeit you might look fantastic doing it. As Michael says in his fishing lectures, "Might as well fish in a mud puddle if you don't know how to judge the water."

In this discussion, we'd like to teach you how to look at water—or rather how to look

Some people look at this and say "nice water."
For serious anglers, this stretch tells a story.

Even a small stream like this can be productive if you read the water. Note the shady banks and larger rocks on the far side.

into the fish's world. Too many casters are surface-centric. It's easy to see why they catch fish only now and then. They are passive rather than active anglers. If you want to get good at this sport, you have to look at the streams, rivers, and lakes the way a fish does. You can't think exactly like a fish since our beloved finned foe has a brain slightly larger than a couple of BBs, but you can learn how a fish will think (or maybe react).

READ ANY GOOD BROOKS LATELY?

Beneath the surface of a brook, river, lake, or stream lies a world most humans barely understand. To be successful at spin casting, you'll need to know more about this elusive, aquatic world. You have to look past your reflection and gaze into the heart and soul of the water. The Zen of fish water, or something like that. Fishing folk call this mystical process seeing beyond the surface.

Reading the surface, or film, of your favorite water can give you an accurate picture of what's going on underneath. We're going to

show you how to become an expert at reading all kinds of water—whether it be stream, river, lake, pond, irrigation canal, or kiddieland pay-by-the-inch trout farm.

THINKING LIKE A FISH: THE FOUR F'S

Fish only do four things. In case you don't know what they are, here's a hint: they all start with the letter F. Can you guess?

1. Feed

2. Fight (for territory)

3. Flee

4. Fool around (i.e., spawn—and don't think we don't know what you're thinking)

In order to make sense of what you read on the surface, you have to know how fish respond to their environment in terms of the four F's. To be a successful angler, you have to train yourself to think like a fish. Every time you see a stretch of water, ask yourself, where will the fish be and why? Which F's are being met in this water?

Can you read this stream? Where are the fish likely to be holding?

Learning to think like a fish doesn't mean you have to jump in the water, grow gills, and start sucking bugs. In fact, this may be a good time to clarify something. We say think like a fish, but we don't mean it literally. Fish aren't really smart (which makes you really feel low when you get skunked as we all do from time to time). Your average fish has a brain about the size of an entrée at a trendy Los Angeles restaurant. What we really mean is this: *We want you to understand fish.* If you understand our dull-witted, but wonderful, finned friends, you'll have a plan and start fishing in water that looks productive every time.

We're going to focus on a fish's feeding habits and moods (feeding is the first and most important of the four F's). We'll talk about when and how fish eat, but most importantly we'll talk about where fish eat.

Fish Food

Stuffing themselves to the gills is what fish do for a living. Understand how and where fish find food and you'll find fish to cast to, which is more than half the battle for the serious angler. Meet a fish's terms, and you can drive a fancy, laser-sharpened hook through his pouting lip with pleasure and style.

Bass often hang close to reeds to feed and flee.

A lunker bass or trout can't head off to Arby's when it needs a snack. It has to hunt. Life in the underwater world is a battle where the fish that eats the most grows the biggest and lives the longest—if it's lucky and careful. Yet, despite the ongoing battle, fish, especially stream fish, are remarkably lazy—they'd rather sit and wait for food to arrive than lift a fin to work at it. Evolution has trained them to exert as little effort as possible to get as much food as possible, which makes sense.

As spin casters, we're not concerned so much with *what* fish eat as with *where* and *how* a fish eats. A spinning lure doesn't look or smell like any single item on the fish's menu. However, it is able to trigger a fish's attack for food response.

Fish Lies

The *fisherman's lie* is the semi-fact-filled whopper—telling your fishing buddies about the one that got away, or stretching the size of the fry you landed. Many a time our nice seventeen-inch browns have grown to twenty-one inches within hours of their release (this is particularly true of fish we happen to photograph at just the right angle—Mike is very good at this). The fisherman's lie is a traditional art form we're proud to be a part of. It's part of our angling heritage.

The *fish's lie,* however, is the term anglers use to describe the place in a river a fish occupies, or holds in, while waiting for the current to bring food. In still water, a lie is the place a fish rests or the place a fish waits to ambush its prey. As you start to read the water, you'll need to look for likely lies the fish could be holding in. Lies can be roughly divided into two categories: a feeding lie and a resting lie.

A feeding lie is a fish's underwater dining room. This is where fish actively feed, making it exceptionally productive water for spin casters to work. It makes sense to spend your fishing time casting to hungry fish. A less productive but sometimes promising place to fish, if you can't find a feeding lie, is a resting lie. This is the fish's bedroom. You won't find a lot of hungry fish here, but you'll sometimes be able to tempt one with an easy midnight meal. Fish in the bedroom are more concerned about safety than food, so they spook easily.

During those occasional times when fish have achieved relative safety or the food is so plentiful they can't resist, they turn their attention to gorging themselves. They feed hard, taking in all the calories they can with as little effort as possible. When they rest, they shut down in safe, often gentle water, still expending as little effort as possible. Though not as productive as a feeding lie, fishing a resting lie sure beats dragging a spinner through empty water, where your chances of catching a fish hover close to the zero mark.

Fish play a deadly lifelong game of king of the hill. The smartest and biggest fish hold in the best lies—eat the best food, sleep in the safest water—by driving away the smaller,

Alan tries to provoke a strike in the resting lie when the feeding shuts down on a hot afternoon.

Fish often feed facing into the current that brings food to them.

weaker fish. A good lie today, unless other conditions change, will be a good lie tomorrow or next week. Fishing the best lies always gives you a crack at the biggest fish. To know where the best lies are, you have to read the water.

Fish Lies in Streams and Rivers

If you were a fish waiting for the current to bring you mouthwatering bits of really good, calorie-injected victuals, where would you wait?

As a stream fish, your version of utopia is water where the current brings the food to you, but where you don't have to battle the current while you wait. You might perch yourself behind a big rock or snag. The current rushes past you and you can see the food coming by, but the structure breaks down the water flow so you expend as few calories as possible holding your position.

An imaginative caster looks for breaks in the water to find good lies: boulders, snags, junk cars, drop-offs, gravel bars, old washing machines, islands . . . anything that disturbs

the flow of the water. Fish rest in the lee water, slip into the fast water for a quick bite, then slide back.

The surface current may be, and often is, very different from the current at the bottom of the stream. Look for whirlpools or swirls of current that might indicate the water on the bottom is broken up—thanks to a rock. Such a place is a probable lie, since the barrier slows the drifting food and breaks up the current.

Two separate current flows are also great places for fish. You'll often have a fast current and a slower one joined together into a *seam*. Fish will hold in the slower current waiting for food to drift by in the faster current.

Fish Lies in Lakes and Still Water

Fish in lakes and still water don't enjoy the same level of room-service luxury that their river and stream counterparts do, but they don't have to deal with calorie-consuming currents. Still-water fish are hunter-gatherers, much like our own ancient ancestors. They patrol for food

Riffles and current seams are prime fish haunts.

when and where it is readily available, then seek shelter the rest of the time.

Natural food sources are most abundant in and around structure. Besides the shelter and safety it offers, bugs, minnows, nymphs, and other prey congregate around shelter to avoid being eaten themselves—at least their odds of being eaten are lower here than in open water. At different times of the day, typically the morning and evening hours, a feast of insects lies on the water's surface.

Active, Passive, and Selective Fish

Fish, especially big fish, are downright moody, and their moods shift fast. One minute a stretch of water might be on fire; the next minute it can be completely shut down. Knowing fish moods helps you work through the swings and stages to consistently catch fish.

Familiarity with fish moods is common among accomplished fly casters but, surprisingly, ignored by spin casters. That's too bad because good fly casters catch a lot of fish. Is

fly tackle really that good? Frankly, feathers, elk hair, and peacock herl alone aren't the reason. Rather, it's the nature of the sport itself. Fly casters, as a rule, understand fish better than do spin casters. If you fly-fish you have to match the hatch, present your lure properly, and read the water, which forces you to think like a fish. Spin casters should take a lesson from their fly casting counterparts and do likewise.

Fisherman categorize feeding behavior in the following manner: active, selective, and passive.

Active. Active or aggressive fish are hungry and ready to eat. They hold in water with an ample supply of food, and they have to get as much of it as they can. Remember, the water they're in and their activity level burn energy (calories), so the pressure is on for them to take in a lot more calories than they expend.

As you'd expect, active fish are the easiest to catch. They're hungry and ready to eat and do so, seemingly, with reckless abandon. When active feeders hit your lure, they usually hit it hard! You could cast a bottle cap stuck on a safety pin and an active feeder might nail it. If you've ever seen a slow fishing day suddenly

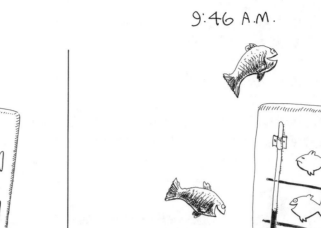

7:32 A.M.   9:46 A.M.

and dramatically pick up—even though your fishing pattern didn't change—you've experienced fish becoming active.

Selective Fish. These fish share most of the same characteristics as active fish, except they are usually honed in on one type of food (often an insect hatch) and little else will satisfy them. You're probably no different. If you're in the mood for KFC Extra Crispy, it doesn't matter how tempting a well-grilled New York steak might sound.

Selective fish are fish with an attitude, fish that turn up their noses at everything—except what they're in the mood for. Often, our persnickety finned friends are feeding on a voluptuous insect hatch, and they'll look at nothing else. It can be hard to tempt them with your offering. Try a different size lure or one that is completely different. When in doubt, go smaller with a softer action. Work with different retrieves. A complete change will sometimes trigger a response.

Selective fish can be frustrating since you see them working the water, but they pay little attention to your presentation. With discriminating fish like these, what you should be looking for is an *opportunistic* eater. You want a fish to step out of its selective paradigm just for a moment and take your lure.

Your best strategy is variety. Tie on different lures more frequently and get a rotation going. Use a smaller size, a different color, a new pattern. If the right lure is in the right place at the right time, a selective fish will decide to take what you are offering. Whatever you do, don't beat yourself up fishing unproductive water. If all else fails, try a different section of water for a while. Come back in an hour. Sooner or later the fish will stop being selective.

Passive Fish. A passive or neutral fish has little interest in food and is dormant. Passive fish hold in safe water that's usually deep and calm. Here a fish can expend as little energy as possible and be somewhat safe from predators above and below. There is usually some sort of structure to hide in or around. Occasionally you can provoke a passive fish into taking your lure. This kind of strike is triggered by aggression, not hunger.

Think about it. How would you react to some wiseacre dragging a triple teaser across your down comforter while you're trying to snooze. Provoking a strike is a good technique, but you frequently have to drag the same lure past the same fish several times. On the whole, however, too many anglers spend too much of their time fishing for passive fish. Your fish finder may be sounding off like a Geiger counter at Chernobyl, but if all those fish are passive, they won't be fighting over your offering.

The Least You Should Know about Fish and Temperature

Every fish has an optimum water temperature zone—sometimes called the thermal belt or thermocline. It is important that you know the preferred temperature of the fish you are seeking. This will help you know where to fish and how.

A fish processes dissolved oxygen. When the water gets warmer and loses that oxygen, the fish seeks, if it can, a more comfortable temperature. If the water gets too warm, a fish literally can't breathe and will die. Warm water curtails feeding activity. The fish has to work hard just to get the minimal amount of oxygen it needs to breathe. For us it would be like sitting in the shade in 122-degree heat; all we'd do is sit and try to fan ourselves. It's no wonder fishing shuts down when the water gets too warm for a fish's comfort.

When water gets too cold it also loses oxygen. During this time, a fish's metabolism (fueled by dissolved oxygen) starts to shut down. It is more difficult, and takes longer, for the fish to digest food. Obviously, a fish can't grow very fast when all its energies are spent trying to breathe instead of searching for food.

Approximate Temperature Guide for Game Fish

These temperatures ranges are only a guide and can vary depending on the altitude, the geographic location, and the climate. You also need to consider available oxygen and food sources.

	Low Range	Optimum	Upper Range
Bluegill	57	70	76
Brook Trout	44	60	70
Brown Trout	45	55–66	73
Crappie (Black)	59	71	75
Lake Trout	41	50–58	62
Largemouth Bass	59	70	75–80
Muskie	55	63	72
Northern Pike	56	64	75
Rainbow Trout	44	49–65	75
Smallmouth Bass	60	65–70	74
Steelhead	39	50	48–59
Sunfish	50	60	70
Walleye	50	67	76
Yellow Perch	59	64	75

THE DIFFERENT WATERS ON A STREAM

A flowing body of water can be broken down into four general types of water: flats, riffles, pools, and runs. Being able to look at a stretch of water and know something about it is a great first step. You won't be just plowing in; you'll be fishing with a plan since different types of water help meet a fish's basic needs. You'll have a better idea about where the fish are.

Let's talk about each type of water and look at the fish it might hold.

Flats

As the name implies, a flat is a stretch of smooth surface water with a relatively flat and smooth bottom (which is partly why the top is smooth). Flats tend to be shallow and easy to wade. Because they're shallow and smooth, you have to be careful when you fish, so fish don't see you. It's also a good idea to use smaller lures that don't splash or displace a lot of water (unless the fish are very aggressive). Also, the rattle of rocks when you walk, wakes from wading, or the shadow of your rod tip can send fish to the nearest cover.

TYPES OF WATER IN A STREAM

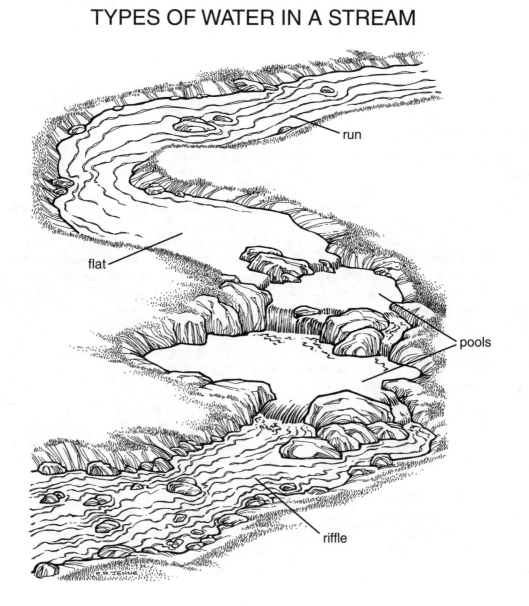

run

flat

pools

riffle

Fish have a natural defense mechanism (Flee, one of the four F's) that tells them to hightail it out of sight whenever they see something moving above the water. Natural selection drilled this into them after eons of ancestors got nailed by eagles, bears, otters, and so on. Fish haven't evolved enough to know that the tip of your fishing rod is a threat, but they have enough neurotic baggage left over from these other hazards that they go ballistic any time they sense movement above.

You'll find lots of fish in flats. Since food is abundant, fish feed with a vengeance. However, these fish can be selective. If, after changing lures a few times, you aren't successful, keep moving. Look for fish near banks and undercuts where several currents meet, where a creek enters, in shadows, and near moss lines. Any sort of structure in a flat can hold fish—a snag, a boulder, a drop-off. Fish will often hold in deeper water and shoot into the flat for a bite before swimming out. If possible, climb a tree or a nearby hill and look for working fish; then cast to these specific fish. Also, if fish are feeding, determining how provides a clue to what they are taking.

Riffles

Riffles are one of the major feeding areas for fish, yet spin casters overlook this water too often. Many aren't aware that fish hold here, some are worried about losing tackle, and some don't know the proper fishing strategy to employ. The water isn't deep, about six inches to

---

Looking for Working Fish: What Does a Splash Really Mean?

When you watch fish, what does it mean?

Head and Tail Activity. When you see lots of heads and tails, it means one thing—the fish are likely feeding just under the surface on some sort of emerging insect. Use a lighter, delicate lure.

In this scenario, Alan always starts with a $\frac{1}{24}$- or $\frac{1}{16}$-ounce Original Rooster Tail (perhaps heavier in larger water) or a $\frac{1}{32}$- or $\frac{1}{16}$-ounce Panther Martin. Michael likes to start with a $\frac{1}{8}$-ounce Super Duper #503 (silver with a red head)—its erratic, twisting side-to-side action doesn't spook fish. Most $\frac{1}{8}$-ounce lures are too heavy for delicate situations, but this lure is an exception. He is also fond of the Original Mepps $\frac{1}{12}$ or $\frac{1}{8}$ ounce with a silver or a red-white blade. Work the lure as slowly as you can, keeping it right under the surface. Try darting it about if a straight retrieve doesn't work. As a rule of thumb, with many exceptions, the closer a fish comes to the surface, the more likely it is to be feeding selectively.

Gulping or Ringing Activity (little or no splash). When all you see is a ring of water, the fish are feeding right on the surface of the water. Fish the same lure you would for head and tail activity. Remember, fish this close to the surface are spooky.

Jumping Activity (coming out of the water). This usually indicates aggressive fish. They are anxious and snagging bugs out of the air or feeding on terrestrials floating on the water. Often, just about anything you throw will attract the fish's attention. If your lure is being ignored, go smaller, try a different action, tie on a different color . . . or walk back to the car for a fly rod.

Working the Deep Water. Fish might be eating some sort of specific emerger hatching in the water, or they're munching on whatever the current is bringing. Either way, when fish are a little deeper, they're less skittish and more likely to take what you are dragging. They are simply less selective. Fish in these waters are more opportunistic, which is good news for spinners.

four feet. However, since the top is broken up and a bit choppy, fish feel relatively safe since they can't be seen from above.

Riffles bring lots of food to waiting fish. Fish here are on the prowl and waiting for food. Spinning in this water is often fast and quick. Frequently, you cast, retrieve, and you're out of the zone. There are often no long retrieves. Still, the fishing can be hot. Fish in this water don't suffer from indecision—even if they are still a little spooky (the water depth will have something to do with this—as a rule, the deeper you go, the less spooky the fish will be). They simply don't have time to carefully examine what they're eating; it's moving by too fast.

When you're fishing a riffle, work through all the water systematically yet quickly—unless you see a working fish. However, pay close attention to any structure or drop-offs you see and watch the edges.

Pools

A pool is the one body of water most of us know about—it's also the water that gets the most fishing attention in the stream, and for good reason since the biggest and the strongest fish call this home. The hogs have monopolized the best feeding areas and holding lies for so long they can go where they want.

A pool is a good place to try your larger tackle. Large fish, as you'd expect, will eat larger dinners. A big fish can move once and gobble something larger, or move a dozen times after smaller food for the same amount of energy. Use spinner patterns that resemble fry, leeches, sculpin, and crayfish.

Pools are slow and deep. The fish in the middle (except in smaller waters) are big . . . but usually holding close to the bottom. These are neutral fish. If the middle isn't producing, work the edges. The active, biggest fish will generally be at the head or the tail of the pool. Mornings and evenings are the best times to fish a pool.

Runs

A run, or glide, is a smooth-flowing stretch of water. The top looks somewhat calm with a riffle or a swirl here or there, but the current is moving along at a good clip. The rocks and structure that provide shelter for fish and the highly oxygenated water create an ideal habitat.

While runs aren't always the best place for a fish to find food, fish here are usually opportunistic and that spells good news for the caster. Getting to know a good glide is one of the great joys of fishing, but it often takes some time since there is so much going on underneath the surface. To successfully fish a run, look for edges, places where two different currents meet, a creek mouth, a moss line, or anything that breaks up the current and provides shelter. Most of the fish will be hugging the bottom, unless there's an insect hatch.

You'll want to literally bang your lure across the floor. Depending on the current and the conditions, you may need a lure with a little more weight. Sure, you'll lose tackle in this water, but it's worth it. We've both caught some excellent fish in this water. When we aren't sure where to cast, we usually start with a run.

"LET'S KEEP THE SPRAY HANDY — BUT I THINK WE'RE OKAY
AS LONG AS HE KEEPS CATCHING FISH."

6
FISHING CREEKS, STREAMS, AND RIVERS
The Secrets of Flowing Water

Stream fishing is one of the great joys of spin casting. Whether you're fishing a small creek in Starr Valley, Wyoming, or a mighty river like the Athabasca in Canada that's nearly a half mile wide, the principles are the same. Fish will seek water that is safe and comfortable, water that provides lots of food with as little effort as possible. The applications, however, are different. In this chapter, let's look at how to fish flowing water, be it large or small.

SMALL CREEKS AND STREAMS

There are few things as glorious as a small stream. A stream has a life and beauty that thrills the soul. There's an incredible immediacy about small stream casting—it's a great test among you, the water, and the fish.

Often-overlooked small waters can yield big fish. We were casting one autumn in some very unlikely water in Starr Valley, Wyoming. At places, you could almost walk across the stream with a big step. Under those undercut banks, we discovered, lurked some very large German brown trout. Almost on cue, fifty yards apart, we hooked two large lunkers within seconds. It was a crisp October day but the sun was shining. All you could hear in the faint breeze was the whining purr of two stressed-out drags on ultralight reels and the rustle of drying willow leaves. It was a day pretty close to heaven.

True, not all small water holds big fish. However, there are more big fish in small streams than what you might think. Certainly the term *big* is relative, and we'll leave you to decide what big is for you, but small water is worth fishing for a number of other reasons.

For one reason, small streams don't get the pressure larger waters get. For another, if there is pressure, it's usually on a few easy-to-get-to holes. You can't fish a small stream effectively unless you're always on the move. The fishing is often dynamic—if one hole is flat, the next one could be hot. The caster who likes to move a lot will rarely have a fishless day on a small stream.

Small waters sometimes hold big fish.

Small Waters: Consider Thy Approach

When a small stream turns fickle, don't head to the 7Eleven for a Big Gulp and a Hostess Cupcake. It's alright to be a little frustrated—there are fish, you've seen them, but they are spooky and selective. Here are a few ideas:

- Go smaller. Go to 2- or 3-pound-test line. Small-water fish can get line sensitive. At the same time, try smaller lures ($\frac{1}{8}$ to $\frac{1}{32}$ ounce).

- Use a lure with a gentler action. While a radical lure might be just the ticket for a less selective, aggressive fish, it will frighten fish on days like this. If you notice that the fish investigate or follow your lure but don't take it, go smaller.

- Don't cast more than once to fish in clear, gentle water. Carefully move on to the broken riffles where fish can't see you.

- Crawl up to the edge of the bank and cast so fish don't see you or your shadow. Tread softly, too, so fish don't hear you.

- If lures aren't working, tie on a small, clear plastic float with four or five feet of leader and drift a grasshopper fly over the likely areas.

Small-stream trout are spooky. Any shadow, including your own, sends fish to the nearest cover. *Work the likely water once carefully—then move on.* Rarely will a lure tempt a small-stream fish after the first presentation. If a fish in a pool is going to take a spinner, it will take it on the first or second cast. Working a pool to death might even prove counterproductive. Not only does it waste time, but you could spook fish, which might alert other fish of your presence in the next good hole. The secret is to cover a lot of water.

It's hard to fish the holes effectively from the bank. Small streams require wading. You can ignore a lot of heavy brush and prevent hanging up in it by walking up the middle of the stream. Also, you won't cast as much of a shadow as when on the bank.

Remember, you want to work the water quickly, but that doesn't mean walk through it quickly. If wading in deeper water, each step should be deliberate. You'll spook fewer fish. If possible, walk around pools after you have fished them, staying in shallower water or even on the stream's edge. Remember, one fish terrorized by your movement can screw up the next hole for you.

Fishing a small stream

SMALL STREAM STRUCTURE

- Look for trout holding and feeding in structured areas of the stream—these areas provide safety, shelter, protection from the current, and, of course, food.

- Stream fish are spooky. Don't let them see you. Your approach and presentation have to be perfect.

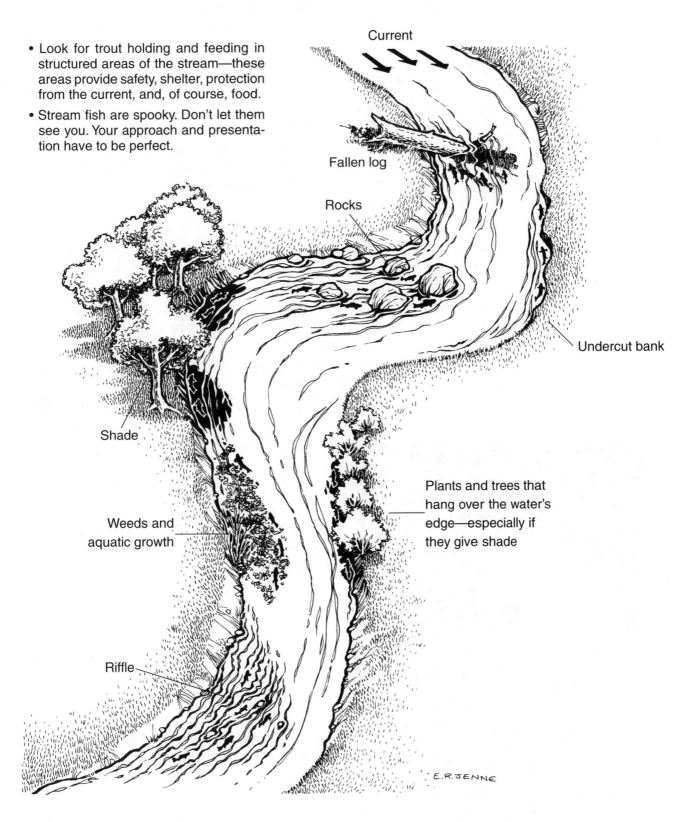

Current

Fallen log

Rocks

Undercut bank

Shade

Weeds and aquatic growth

Plants and trees that hang over the water's edge—especially if they give shade

Riffle

E.R.JENNE

Wading also allows you to cast upstream and get a better retrieve on your lure when you work through a hole. By positioning your rod to the right, left, or in front of you, you can control your lure and keep it in the strike zone—something hard to do from the bank. Feeding fish love undercuts, shady edges, and side pools—areas virtually impossible to fish if you're not in the water up close and personal.

Being in the water below the fish reduces your shadow, but it also helps you adjust your lure speed. It's OK to retrieve the lure at angles in the water. If a fish is aggressive, it will attack a spinner from almost any angle. And frankly, when you're facing the obstacles of stream fishing, it's tough to always get that perfect cast. Nevertheless, remember that when these fish are in their feeding zones, it's often

in shallower water and it won't take much to send them to the shadows.

The more closely you can approximate the feeding patterns of a fish, the more fish you'll catch. Like a fly caster, your presentation has to be very good if you're going to tempt a fish from behind a rock or a snag. Work your spinner like a real piece of food.

Consider the fish's position. It's likely holding just behind a rock or branch that breaks up the flow of the water, and it's watching upstream for dinner. If your spinner is moving with the current, traveling just faster than the water so it flutters and moves properly, it's in the best position to attract fish.

In quick water, you may have to retrieve quickly and the cast may be short. Novice small-stream casters wonder if the lure moves too fast. How will the fish get it? Unlike trout in slower water, these fish have survived making quick decisions. Food comes to them every day in the fast current. Your lure retrieved a little faster than the water flow won't be too fast. If it looks good, a fish will take it.

Identify the water you think is prime. Then, over-cast. You don't want to plop your lure in front of the fish. Cast it above so it is in position and working when it hits the prime water. Dropping your lure in front of its nose is a great way of spooking it to the next pool.

Small streams often reward the determined angler.

LARGE STREAMS

Fishing a large body of water can be very overwhelming. There's so much water, it's hard to know where to start. With a smaller stream, you know there will be some dead water, but you're at least reassured that you'll be hitting some good pockets and some fish, from time to time. With a large river, you could fish all day and never know if you were dragging your hardware in front of a fish's nose. To fish a large stream effectively, you need to cast with a plan. A randomly flung lure will land you a few fish

Knowing where to cast is the first step to successful fishing on a large river.

and foul many fishing holes. How do you work large waters intelligently? You call on a trusty fan cast or downstream swing.

A fan cast across allows you to systematically fish water across the stream from you. Identify the strike zone; then cast upstream of the closest edge of the zone. Let your lure drift through the strike zone at a shallow depth. Cast to the same spot again, but this time let the lure drift deeply through that section. Repeat this action as you fan consecutive casts to farther sections of the strike zone, fishing each section shallow and then deep.

A fan cast above is about the only effective way to work water flowing toward you. Standing downstream of the strike zone, cast upstream of the zone and retrieve your lure through the zone just faster than the current. Work from one side of the strike zone to the other, fanning your casts so you cover the entire pocket. Work each section shallow and then deep. When fan casting above, you might want to use a heavier lure, which will sink sufficiently even as you retrieve it faster than the current.

A downstream swing allows you to selectively fish water below you. In this cast, you use the current to swing the lure into a pocket you can't cast to directly. Cast downstream to the far side of your strike zone and let the current swing your lure into the strike zone. Retrieve your lure after it crosses the zone. Again, use consecutive shallow and deep casts to systematically fish each section of the pocket. We've found the downstream swing an effective cast for salmon, steelhead, and any fish that holds in pockets in large streams and rivers.

Do Some Homework

While we'll teach you a few things about reading big water, it never hurts to glean all the information you can from the locals—from the folks in the store, people you meet on the street, or other anglers on the water (especially those catching fish).

Not all the information you get will be good, but at least it gives you a place to start. If you learn, for example, that pike stack up like cordwood next to grassy banks in the spring, you'd be foolish not to fish there. Don't ignore local publications geared to specific local waters (or magazines and books on the same subject).

FAN CAST ACROSS

Use to work the water in front of you.

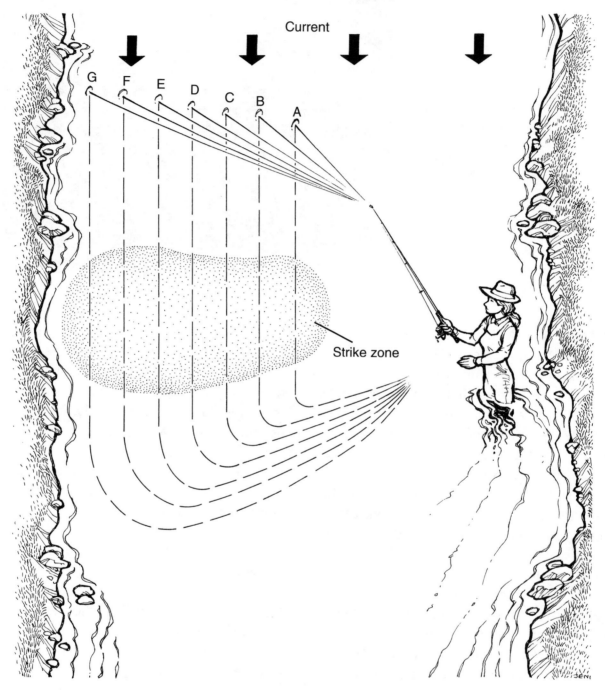

- Fan the water in front, working water off the edge of the bank.
- Work the water carefully so you can present your lure to waiting fish. Make a short cast upstream and work the edge of the strike zone. When the lure becomes even with you, drop the rod tip and follow the hardware. For the best coverage, work each section shallow and deep. The first cast should be shallow, the second cast allowed to sink (you may need to cast a little farther upstream).

FAN CAST ABOVE

Use to work the water above you.

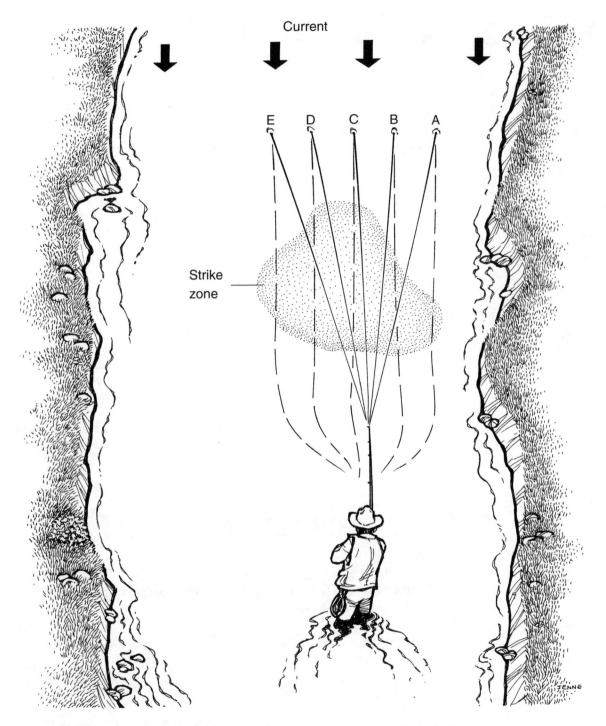

- To work the water above you, bring the spinner to you just ahead of the current.

- Work each section twice. The first cast above the pool should be shallow; let the second cast sink deeper. Wait before bringing the lure in and retrieve it just faster than the current. Cast farther upstream if you need more time to get your lure down.

DOWNSTREAM SWING

Use to work the water below you.

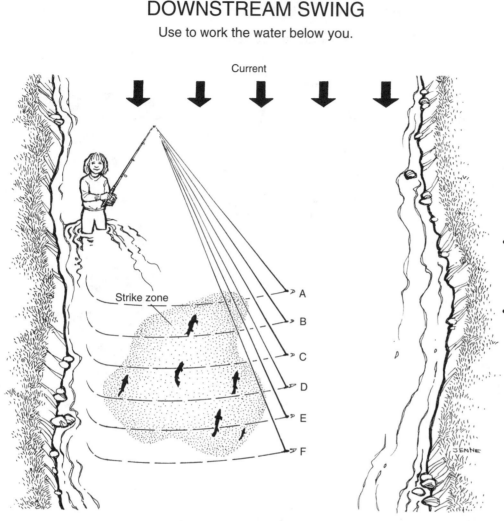

Current

Strike zone

A
B
C
D
E
F

JENNE

- To fish a pocket or a strike zone below you, use the downstream swing.

- Identify the strike zone and create an imaginary grid. Start at the top (A) and let your lure swing through the zone—once shallow, once deep. Then cast a little farther (B) and let your lure drift and flutter through the grid. Continue until you've covered all the good water.

Larger Waters: Fish the Banks

Don't get intimidated by big water or frustrated that you're not floating in a nice drift boat instead of wading. Don't look longingly to the waters out there. If you're on the bank, you're standing right next to some great fishing.

A wader can be a very successful angler since the best water often isn't in the middle of the river. Notice where most of the boats are? That's right, they're fishing the edges. Just think, you're fishing it for free. The guy in the boat is paying $200 or more for the boat ride.

It's true that a drifter, with the oarsman holding the boat, can get a better drift or an angle, but that doesn't mean you have to go away empty-handed. Bank on the banks—that's where the fish are.

- Good water is often *right next to* the edge! Don't overlook this water or plunge into it to wade to another hole until you've fished it or are sure fish aren't holding there.

- When you start wading, pay attention to water next to the bank. There is nothing wrong with casting onto the bank and pulling your lure into the water as you retrieve it. You'll catch a lot of fish if you use this technique.

- The outside bend of a river almost always holds fish since it collects more food and the current is slower. Not only do fish feed on terrestrials that have dropped in the water and insects pushed from the main current to the bank, they also take advantage of the shade.

Gear for the Big Water

On a larger river, especially if there is a possibility of larger fish, you'll want to have the right gear or you'll be very disappointed if you do hook a large fish.

• Most the time (unless we're making long casts or are fishing for salmon or steelhead), we prefer a 6-foot medium-action rod with a stiff butt and a fast tip. A fast tip allows you to feel subtle differences between the bottom, the action of your lure, and a possible strike.

• A good reel with over 200 yards of line (from 4- to 12-pound-test depending on the fish and river conditions). You want enough line so a large fish won't spool you (especially if the fish gets in the current).

• A good drag. Remember not to set the drag too tight. You should be able to strip out line with one hand. If you have doubt, set your drag on the loose side. Anglers lose fish because of drags set too tight.

• If the fish are spooky on a sunny day, switch to bronze or gold hardware. Sometimes silver flashes too much and scares the fish.

READING THE WATER

A river is a big body of water that seems overwhelming when you first look at it. Where are you going to start? Think like a fish.

Don't think of a river as a big body of water. Look at it as a collection of small streams. In this sea of streams, there are also large and small pools, pockets, seams, and riffles. Select a section of water and study it. Ask yourself what Alan calls the *River Wheres*:

• Where would a fish find food?

• Where would a fish find shelter from the current while searching for food?

• Where would a fish likely hold when it wasn't feeding?

• Where would a fish hide?

• Where could a fish find food, seek shelter from the current, and hide all at the same time?

To fish a river effectively, you have to break up the water into fishable parts. There is a lot of water to cover, so you have to come up with a battle plan. If you fish with a consistent plan,

Every stretch of water presents a new opportunity. Make sure you fish with a plan.

BREAK THE RIVER DOWN: FISH A GRID

Identify the strike zones or pockets.

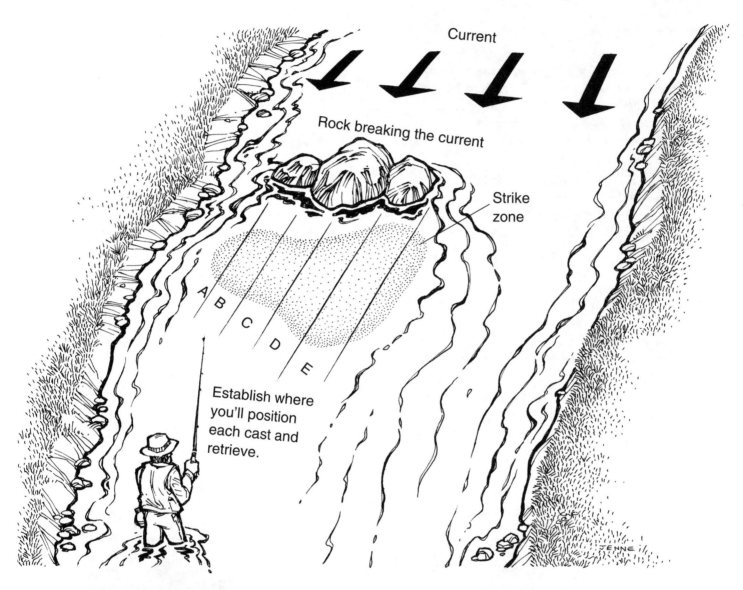

Current

Rock breaking the current

Strike zone

A B C D E

Establish where you'll position each cast and retrieve.

- Before you cast, plan how you'll fish the water.

- Identify where the strike zone is. You'll want to cast above the zone. Establish an imaginary grid and cast to it so you can cover the water systematically.

you'll catch fish consistently (and be part of the 10 percent who catch 90 percent of the fish).

Plan Your Approach

You've decided where the fish will be. At first you'll want to fish all the likely spots. But don't be so rigid in your plan that you aren't flexible. If you discover after working the water that you're catching most of your fish in the pockets behind rocks, stay with that approach. It's obvious that you should focus on this type of water until the fishing flattens. It would be silly to work other waters.

Look over a stretch of water and consider how you'll fish each area you think holds fish. Think about which type of cast will put your lure in the pocket you want to work. Then systematically cast to or drift your lure through the strike zone. If you have a plan, you aren't going to foul water as you fish. Once on the Green River in eastern Utah, we were doing a seminar with two high-rolling computer executives from Hong Kong and New York. Both men were equally equipped, but by the second day, one was catching a lot more fish. The other was getting frustrated. We spent half an hour watching him.

Both men had the same rod and reel. Both had about the same casting skills and understanding of spin casting. Since the man who was frustrated was paying our salary, we watched him carefully. It didn't take very long to figure it out. The man in question was very good at identifying areas that held fish, but he gave no thought to how he approached each area he fished. He fished the first section well, but he ended up fouling four out of six of the places he fished.

Let's say there are five places on a patch of water you want to fish. Plan how you'll fish each one so your approach or how you fish one section will not affect another. This all sounds very obvious, but it's a very common mistake. It's as important as keeping your eye on the ball in golf.

When you wade the big water, do it safely. A wading staff offers security when fording water, crossing slick surfaces, and casting in swift water. Most weigh about nothing, fold neatly, and double as a hiking stick when you're getting into an area. It's important to exercise common sense around water in general, but on big water especially, extra caution can save you from, at the very least, a dunking.

7
LAKES AND PONDS
The Secrets of Fishing from Boat and Shore

Spinning on lakes and ponds is different from stream fishing—not better or worse, just different. Although calm-water fishing and stream fishing have some similarities, you'll need to account for one major difference (if you like catching fish): with few exceptions, in a stream the current brings the food. The fish positions itself in the current and waits for the watery conveyer belt to bring dinner. But in a lake or a pond, there is no current; a fish has to hunt or patrol for its dinner.

In this chapter, we'll talk about fishing lakes and ponds from boat or shore. Although a boat is probably best most of the time, it's not necessary for successful fishing. We've fished plenty of high alpine lakes where packing in a boat was out of the question. When it's shore fish or don't fish, you should know enough tricks to successfully play any hand you're dealt.

A lake or a pond has a lot of open water to cover. You could spend days and only cast to a small portion of it. Successful anglers know

Michael is working his lure just fine from shore.

where to start. Remember, fish hold in deep water where there's security but fish feed most often near shore. As in stream fishing, look for seams—where feeder streams enter or where there is some structure.

THREE TYPES OF WATER

Every lake or pond is different, but for the most part, the water is usually divided up between the deeper sections and the shallower flat sections with some sort of a transition section between the shallow and deep. You can catch fish in each area.

Shallows

Fish feed most actively and aggressively in the shallower water, from one to twelve feet deep and commonly flat or gently sloping. Depending on the lake, this flatter water around the shoreline may extend a few feet or a hundred yards before dropping into the transition section. At times it might drop right into the deep water.

As a rule, the best place to start fishing is where the fish are feeding—often near the shore. Many casters err by working too far out at first, especially in the spring and fall when the water close to shore is prime. They plop down their tackle box, start casting for the cen-

TYPES OF WATER IN A LAKE OR POND

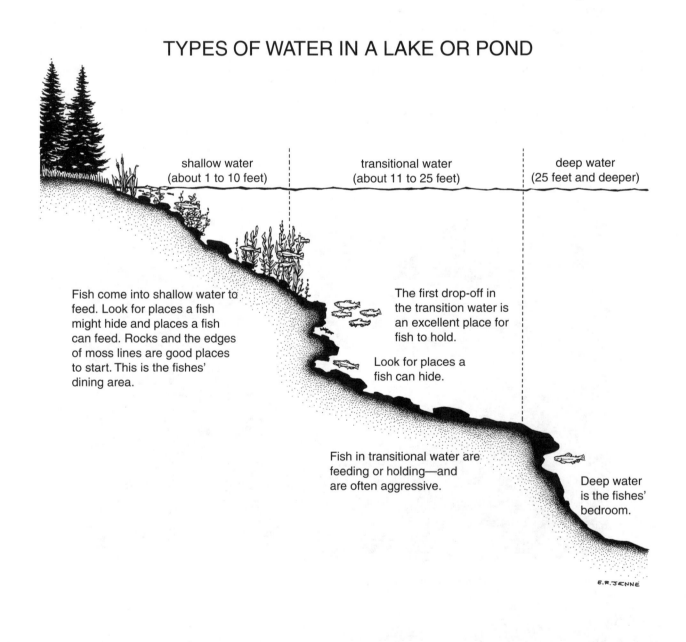

shallow water (about 1 to 10 feet)

transitional water (about 11 to 25 feet)

deep water (25 feet and deeper)

Fish come into shallow water to feed. Look for places a fish might hide and places a fish can feed. Rocks and the edges of moss lines are good places to start. This is the fishes' dining area.

The first drop-off in the transition water is an excellent place for fish to hold.

Look for places a fish can hide.

Fish in transitional water are feeding or holding—and are often aggressive.

Deep water is the fishes' bedroom.

E.R.JENNE

ter of the lake for all they're worth, and wonder why they aren't catching enough fish.

Take a few minutes and watch the shallow water for fish activity. If you can get above the lake and look down, so much the better. A few minutes of looking pays off in more fish.

Transition Zone

Fish hold in the transition water (usually ten to twenty-five feet deep) between the flat, sloping shallow water and the deep stuff, or they move between the shallow and deep water in feeding lanes. In transition water, the flat sloping of the shallow water starts to shelf and drop off quickly into the deep water. The only tricks are locating it and being able to cast out to it.

Transition water is easy to identify if it's close to shore. If you can look down on the lake, watch for the transition zone where the water changes color and becomes darker. If you need to fish the transition water, you may have to move to a spot where you can cast to it from the bank. If the transition zone is a hundred yards out, you won't reach it from shore.

Deep Water

The deeper water can be anything over twenty or thirty feet deep, although it can reach several hundred feet deep. Here the fish are passive unless the water temperature drives most of the aquatic life deep for the summer.

Here Comes the Sun

Use the sun to your advantage when fishing lakes and ponds.

Fishing in the early morning and late evening, especially on lakes, is often great. There's no wind, making locating and casting to the fish easier, and the fish seem to be more active. Often, good hatches come off the surface, which hasn't yet been whipped by the daily winds.

One of the main reasons for the good fishing, however, has to do with light.

Fish don't like ultraviolet (UV) rays. For millions of years, they've known something we're just learning: watch those sun rays. As the sun climbs, fish shy away from the rays (unless feeding conditions are ideal). They hang in the shade, in deeper water, or around structure. Besides not wanting a California tan, fish are more vulnerable to enemies when the sun is directly on the water. Some experts even suggest that trout simply don't like the feel of UV rays on their delicate skin and fins. For whatever reason, they will frequently avoid the sun unless really tempted by food.

In evening and morning, when the UV rays are low in the sky, fish will be more aggressive and more likely to work the top water (if there's food action) since they don't feel so vulnerable. This is one reason why you also see more fish activity on the surface on a cloudy day.

Rock points are great places from which to fish.

Most the time, the fishing in this area is average to marginal. Don't be fooled, however. The deepest water may not be in the middle of the lake but near the edge.

TIMES AND SEASON

If you are fishing in the springtime after ice-off, the shallower water will be warmer than the deeper water and will naturally draw fish. The water temperature will be comfortable, and the warmer water will be alive with food so fish can put on a spring feed. At this time, fish will often hold around any structure in the shallow or transitional water full-time.

If you don't see working fish or obvious structure, or you see so much structure it's confusing, and you're not sure where to start, try a trick Alan learned in his Eagle Scout days. Take out your compass and find dead north. Unless there is a huge rock face, a swamp, or a lot of trees to throw things off, head to the northwest part of the lake. During spring and fall, this water often gets the best sun, so it warms quickly and holds more fish.

SHORE FISHING IN THE SHALLOWS

When you fish the shallows, you fish to hungry fish in their own kitchens. Keep in mind, a fish in shallower water is also a fish more vulnerable to enemies. Because the water is shallower and there is less structure, these fish are very spooky and bolt for deeper water at any sign of danger—like a lure splashing down nearby.

Take the obvious precautions. Don't cast a long shadow on the water, especially a moving shadow. Don't stand where cruising fish can see you. Don't throw a spinner so big it scares the fish.

To a fish, structure like this might as well have a lit-up Motel 6 sign attached.

When you are casting, remember that some waters are more prime than others. Even if you have the best gear in the world, throwing it in the wrong place only gives you casting exercise. If we can't see the fish and aren't sure where they are (no obvious splashes or rings), we look for these indicators:

- Structures such as a boulder, a partly submerged snag, or a floating log give fish a lot of security. A fish can hold there for a long nap or hide between periods of feeding.

- Shelves and drop-offs are prime holding areas. Fish have the safety that the deeper water around the shelf can bring, but they can monitor the shallows, too. This water also may be a temperature buffer if the shallow water is uncomfortable. The water right before shelves and drop-offs can be alive with aquatic organisms that fish thrive on.

- Feeder streams or creeks that bring food and oxygenated water into the lake are also prime locations. Fish will patrol the mouths of even very small feeder streams. Also, the stream's riffle helps hide the fish in the shallow water.

CASTING A SPOOKY SHADOW

- Points of land or inlets are natural breaks in the water that concentrate food and are always good places to fish. Points also allow you to cast over much more water without moving.

- Shorelines are prime areas to cast for feeding fish. Cast parallel to shore. Don't cast straight out into the middle of the lake unless you have good reason to do so. Try to wade out a little ways or stand on a rock or small peninsula to keep your lure in productive water longer.

You don't fish lakes for very long before the wind comes up. Generally, the wind starts to build between 11:00 A.M. to 1:00 P.M. and ends sometime during the late afternoon. The lake's smooth, glassy surface turns choppy and the fishing might slow down, but that's no reason to put up the rod. In hot weather, wave action lowers the water temperature slightly and helps oxygenate the water. In the summer, fish will still feed during the wind. When the wind blows terrestrial insects onto the water, the fishing can be hot.

If possible, keep the wind in your face. The wind will whip the waves and push the insects and other aquatic food toward you. Sometimes a choppy surface gives a fish the courage to come into really shallow water to feed on insects the wind has blown in. Try working a Rooster Tail across the water. If this doesn't produce results, cast deeper and work the lure off the bottom. Under these conditions, it's best to use a little larger lure so you can cast into the wind.

SHORE FISHING IN DEEP WATER

If you've worked the shallow water with little luck, try casting farther out to where the fish are. It's okay to tie on a bigger lure if needed. If your smaller lure is heavy enough to cast, you might continue to try it. You can wait the fish out—they'll be in the kitchen sooner or later—but you're not that sort of angler. You're going to get in their faces (and we love you for it).

Getting Your Lure Out Far Enough. If you are having a hard time getting your small lure to the water you want to fish, tie on some weight. Thread on an egg sinker above the lure, or tie your lure and 14 inches of leader to a swivel. Put the sinker above the swivel. An egg sinker is best because the line floats freely through the body and you can feel the strike faster. Egg sinkers won't twist your line.

Work the Feeding Lanes. Identify possible feeding lanes and cast beyond them, working the lure systematically to cover the most productive water. For your first series of casts, work the top water (if there is fish activity on the surface, you'll want to continue fishing the surface awhile longer). Always start with the top water, and begin with a slow retrieve.

If you don't get a pickup after a volley of casts, vary the speed of your retrieves. Experiment. Some days fish will want it slow, fast, or irregular. Never quite having it wired is what keeps fishing so exciting. The second you think you're the best thing on the water, the playing field—perhaps we should say the fish's playing field—shifts.

Get Your Lure Deeper. So the surface isn't producing and you've covered the feeding zones. Fish may be hugging the bottom or at a certain depth—maybe above or below the thermocline. The best way to find them is by counting down in intervals. Depending on the weight and shape of your lure (obviously, heavy lures sink faster, and the action on some lures causes them to flutter down slowly), wait a few counts before you reel in.

We usually work in intervals of ten. Cast, count to ten, and retrieve. We do this over the likely water. Then we try intervals of twenty, thirty, forty, and so on. If we start hanging up on structure, we go up a few counts. At the same time we'll play with the retrieve. This seems like a lot of work, and it is, but it produces fish.

Fishing the Shallows: What You Know Can Help You

Shallows are often a fish's smorgasbord. Learning about them and about what's happening on the lake will help you catch fish.

- **In the spring (March, April, May, or early June depending on the location of the lake), trout move into the shallows for several reasons: 1) shallow water warms up first; 2) as a result of the warmth, insects hatch; and 3) weed beds start to grow, which provide shelter and food-rich habitat for fish.**

- **In the summer as the water warms and the weeds grow, other food sources develop in the weeds, most importantly, damselfly and dragonfly nymphs and the minnows and small fish that feed on these insects.**

When in doubt, look for weedlines and other kinds of structure to find fish.

GETTING TO THE FISH

First things first. You made it to the lake, you have your equipment, you have some tackle. Now you have to find where the fish are and figure out how to get to them. Knowing the lake helps, but that alone won't always be enough. In spite of all the great shore-fishing tips we just gave you, we admit that fishing from good ol' terra firma doesn't always cut it.

Fish don't stay still; they move to meet their temperature, shelter, and food needs. The shore where you caught a freezer-load of fish in May might be dead water in August. It's usually best to get out on the water. There are many ways—a boat, a tube, a canoe, a kayak, or a raft you tied together with nylon rope. It doesn't matter how fancy or humble your floating device is, you just have to get to where the fish are.

Where to Begin

If you can, talk to locals and research the water you're about to fish. Then, using what you know about reading water and fish habi-

tat, you won't go into battle blind. A topographic map of the lake, if you can get one, will pay many dividends.

It doesn't matter how humble your floating device is, any boat will get you closer to the fish.

STYLIZED TOPOGRAPHIC MAP OF A LAKE

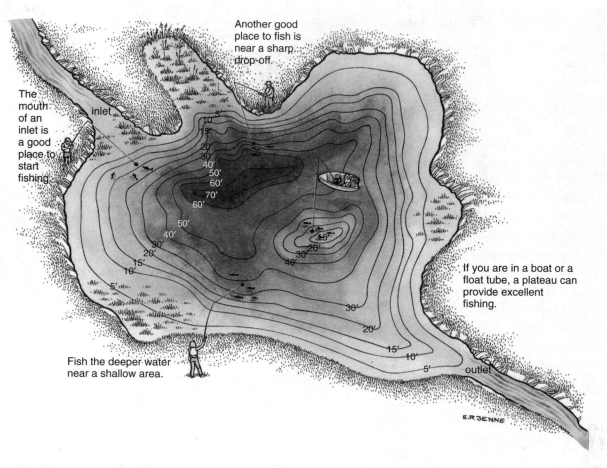

Another good place to fish is near a sharp drop-off.

The mouth of an inlet is a good place to start fishing

inlet

If you are in a boat or a float tube, a plateau can provide excellent fishing.

Fish the deeper water near a shallow area.

outlet

E.R.JENNE

A good friend of Michael's, Steve Partridge, is one of the best fishermen in the country. "I'd trade your front seat in hell for a good map," he said one afternoon. "I can almost tell you where the fish are at any time of the year by looking at a map of the lake."

Steve is right. A map will show you how the bottom of the lake looks. It will show you the plateaus that will yield fish in the summer. It will show you where shelves and drop-offs are. It will help you figure out weed beds and points. In short, a good map can save you a week or two's worth of experimenting.

Work the Points. As with shore fishing, perhaps the best place to start trolling for any game fish is around a point. Feeding fish tend to congregate around points and are aggressive, active, hungry, and lusting for your lure. Because points extend into the body of water, not only are they good hunting grounds but also are often closer to deeper, safer water.

Water depth around a point will vary; it's often deep along the sides and shallow where the point extends into the water. Read the water. What depth and what part seems to provide a fish with the most F's? Some points are large and sweeping. Where do you start? That depends on the time of the year, the water temperature, the variety of food fish are taking, and the type of game fish you are after. Don't ignore any obvious structure somewhere around the point.

Unless you have a good idea where to start, or you're using a fish finder, work all the water and the various depths around the point to locate the fish. Think in broad terms, cover the water, and then focus when you find your finned prey.

FINDING FISH ON A LAKE
The best places to look.

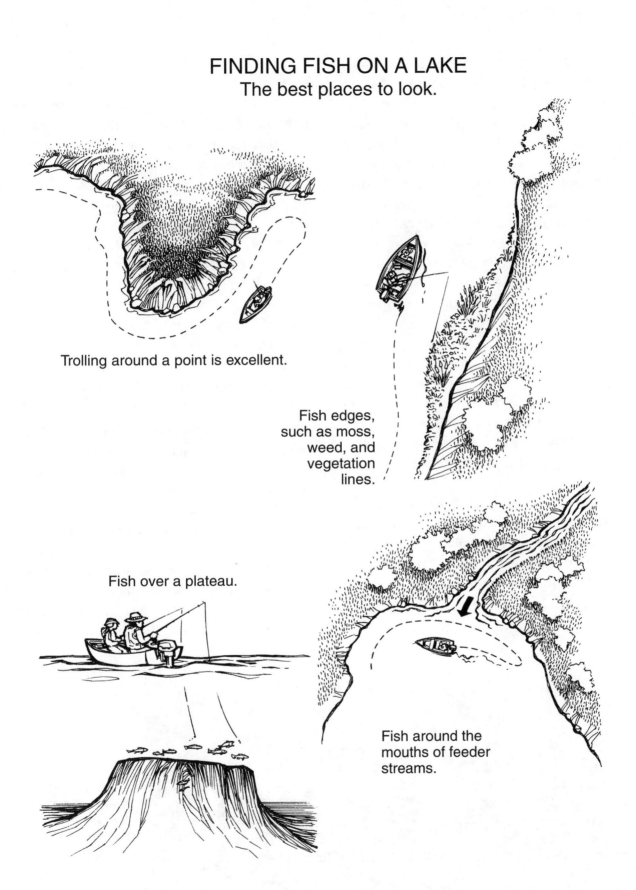

Trolling around a point is excellent.

Fish edges, such as moss, weed, and vegetation lines.

Fish over a plateau.

Fish around the mouths of feeder streams.

Work the Plateaus. A plateau is a fish oasis— and the caster's holy grail. Fish love plateaus and hold on them, especially when the water gets warm or cold. On plateaus not far from the surface, fish hold, aggressive and waiting to attack small fry overhead. This is a favorite trick of the largemouth bass. When fishing shallower plateaus or humps, don't forget to work the edges. A bigger, heavier, more radical lure is just the ticket for a trophy lunker.

In deeper water, hump-resting fish are generally neutral, but they can change their fishy minds if you dangle the right piece of hardware near them. For kicks, watch these fish on a fish finder as you dangle a variety of lures. This will give you a good idea what they like. When you're after resting fish in this situation, reduce your lure size after you've made a pass or two without arousing the interest of your prey. Bigger isn't better. In fact, most folks with lures too big scare neutral fish and turn them off. Smaller is better.

Once you've found a plateau with a fish finder or a map, the next problem is finding it again on a body of water that looks uniform on the surface. With a map, you can triangulate the plateau from familiar points.

Work the Weed Beds and Moss Lines. "There are few better places to fish than a damn fine moss line," Alan always says, the true nature of his largemouth bass alter ego coming out. Nevertheless, bass don't have the exclusive rights to moss lines. Trout love them. Any predator surfs the vegetation for a tender treat of minnow or bug a la carte.

At certain times of the year (usually spring and fall), fish will hold in this water. In the summer when the water is warm and the oxygen levels are low, feeding fish will haunt this water for a meal but won't hold in it. Morning and evening (or after dark where legal) when the weather gets warm are the best times to fish. Watch the water temperature.

Spring, summer, and autumn are great times to focus on trolling the deeper, open-water side of the vegetation. Experiment with lure depth. If there's a chance of snagging, try a weedless hook.

Work the Mouths of Streams and Creeks. The mouths of even small creeks are excellent places to fish for several reasons. Remember a stream with a current is a great boon to fish used to patrolling for every drop of food they've eaten. It might be nice to hold just off the mouth of the stream and let some food come to them instead of the other way around. Don't miss a chance to swing a lure through such water.

Larger fish will either feed off surprises the current has brought to the lake or off smaller

Fishing from a boat is not only fun, it's probably the most productive way to cover a lot of water.

Odds and Ends for the Boat

Needle-nose pliers are useful, especially if you're using treble hooks. They also help you release the fish quickly and keep you from getting hooked.

A bail bucket is a necessity for any boat, especially a small one. A cut-up bleach jug works nicely. A sponge for getting water out of those corners is also nice.

A backpacking-style towel (anything lightweight and fast drying) soaks up, sops up, or mops up. These little towels absorb about nine times their weight in water and then release about 90 percent after a quick twist. We used Cascade Designs Pack Towels on our last trip to Canada. We used them to mop out the boat, to wipe off pike-slimy hands, and after solar showers. They were so handy, our friend Kasey offered us $25 for Alan's.

fish that are themselves feeding off the current. In cool weather the flowing water will often be a little warmer than the pond or lake, so fish will hold near the mouth to warm up.

Conversely, in the summer, flowing water is frequently cooler, and fish will hold near it to be in a more comfortable zone. And even if

the stream and lake are the same temperature, the oxygen-rich flowing water draws fish.

TROLLING TO CATCH FISH

Some folks love to troll and have made it an art form. Some find it about as exciting as watching the grass grow. Whatever your reasons, trolling is, at least, a great way to locate where fish are on a body of water. It's also a great way to catch fish.

In our dynamic duo, Michael is the master troller—trolling both for enjoyment and to catch fish. Alan trolls, but only to locate fish so he can try and catch them by another method, if possible. The exception for Alan is open-water salmon fishing; trolling is the only way to go.

You've got to get the hardware to the fish. Consider a few trolling postulates.

1) Unless you luck out, most fish will be more or less neutral, or at best semiaggressive, in the thermocline. Only an aggressive fish will shoot off after a lure, and you can't count on the fish being aggressive (although if properly presented, your lure can make a fish more aggressive). Remember, fish don't waste energy foolishly chasing hardware.

More gear doesn't always translate into more fish, but why take chances?

2) Don't waste your time trolling dead water.

3) Because your lure is moving rapidly when you troll, it needs to be close to the fish to peak its interest. The closer it is, the more likely the fish will take your offering.

4) Different lures perform differently at different speeds—be aware of these differences and troll accordingly. Hang a lure in the water by the boat and watch its action. If it's not moving, crank up the speed a notch.

5) If you are trolling deep, use a small-diameter line to reduce line drag.

Boat Speed and Boat English

You need to be aware of boat speed at all times. How fast or slow you need to troll varies with the time of the year, the species you are after, the mood of the fish, and the lure you choose. How you manipulate the boat in the water also has something to do with it. We call it "boat English."

Pay attention to your trolling speed. If you're catching fish, keep doing the same thing. If you're not, experiment. There's nothing mystical or magical about it. Varying motor speed moves the lure up and down and gives it added action. Even after you've found that perfect speed, kick it in neutral occasionally or pick up the RPM to add some variety.

One time we were at Flaming Gorge with our friend Steve Partridge. We were trolling over a series of plateaus that afternoon. We can't remember what the exact RPMs were, but when we were at an exact number, we were all into hook-ups at once. Something about that exact speed drew fish like flies to honey. If we got off by a few hundred RPMs, nothing.

On a calm lake, it's easy to keep all variables constant. You might find the right combination in the morning when the lake is flat, only to go bust in the afternoon. However, when the wind comes up like it does most every day, you have to adjust. A wind at your back will speed you up; a wind in your face will slow you down. Slow down or speed up to compensate for the wind and chop.

When trolling, you can control the action of the lure with boat speed and positioning. Motor speed and turning make the lure go deeper or shallower, swing left or right. If you turn the boat to the left, the lure on the right of the boat (the outside of the circle) will speed up and go shallower; the lure on the left (the

BOAT ENGLISH

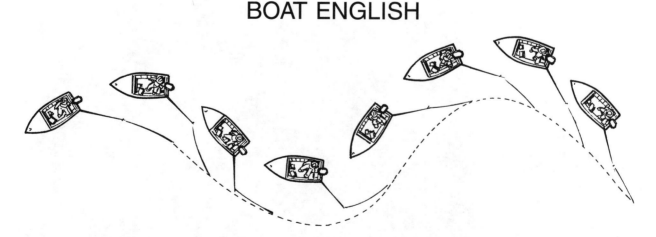

It's rarely effective to troll in a straight line. You cover more water trolling in "S" curves. This technique also keeps your line more isolated from motor noise, and it puts good action on your lure.

inside of the circle) will slow down and go deeper. Certainly, how tight you turn determines the lure speed. Watch the angle of the line. Shoot for a forty-five-degree angle.

It's not unusual to find that fish on a given day seem to favor one turn or another. Discovering this is half the battle. It's a big mistake to troll in a straight line unless you're working a structure or a moss line. It's better to weave back and forth with the boat to give the lures some realistic action. The up-and-down movement of the lure better imitates the baitfish's natural movements.

Depth

You have to find the depth at which the fish are feeding or resting. If you have a fish finder, some of your work is done for you. The only trick is making the fish bite. You can watch your lure on the screen and know within inches if you're in the right zone—and if fish are there. An electronic gadget like this is handy, but people can still catch fish without one.

More than once we've dropped a thermometer attached to marked twine over the edge to find the water temperature at certain depths. A thermometer is a very handy tool for lake fish-

ing and for streams and rivers, too. It can help you find the optimal water for fish.

One shortcut, especially if you're at a new lake, is to ask the dockhand or other anglers with fish at what depth they've been catching fish. In moments, you'll have an idea at what depth to begin your investigation. Mind you, don't ask where successful anglers caught fish—that's an open invitation to lie like a rug. If you simply ask what depth, you'll probably get the truth. Or, if you see someone trolling by with a fish finder, ask how deep the fish are. After a few times, fibbing and semidrunk responses aside, you'll have an idea where to start. Even without our fish finder, we can get focused pretty quickly.

Once you find fish, make sure to keep your hardware at the right depth. Many trollers discover where the fish are and think they're fishing to them, but they're not. They're fishing over or under the thermocline. You've got to keep the lure positioned!

Pay constant attention to boat speed and boat English as you work through a likely area. Most of the time, unless you have a downrigger, getting deep enough is usually the problem. As you troll, the lure drifts up, which is a con-

A portable fish finder is a handy tool that locates fish in a body of water.

FINDING FISH
Locate the thermocline and fish there.

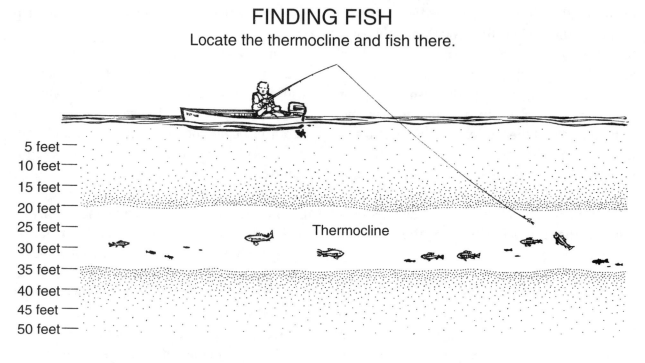

5 feet —
10 feet —
15 feet —
20 feet —
25 feet —
30 feet —
35 feet —
40 feet —
45 feet —
50 feet —

Thermocline

Since nature made fish look up better than down, run your lure a few feet above them to get their attention.

stant problem and one you'll continually have to check. To prevent this, assume a more radical boat English, giving the lure on the lee side time to drop.

Another technique, depending on the weight of the lure and how far you want to go down, is to put the motor into neutral. For a small drop, a few seconds will do. For a big drop, depending on the size of the lure, stay in neutral a minute or more. One of our most successful trolling methods on Flaming Gorge and Fish Lake in Utah or Flathead Lake in Montana is to drop the lure for at least a minute right before we go into the sweet spot. We start lower than the thermocline, but the lure comes up on an incline, and for at least some time, we know we're in the thermocline. You can also couple this, dropping the motor in neutral, when you do some boat English.

Here's a hint: when you find a group of fish, perhaps around a plateau or an excellent section of structure, mark it. You can buy mark-

ers or make them out of old pieces of Styrofoam with a weight and a length of string.

Best Lure Choice. It's really difficult to determine a perfect lure for trolling. A lot has to do with the conditions. It makes sense to go with a heavier lure that will sink faster when you want some depth. However, sometimes a smaller lure, one that's hard to get down, is a better choice for less aggressive fish.

Selecting a trolling lure is like searching for a soul mate—it's a careful process. Perhaps, too, a lure isn't as critical as getting the right depth and action.

Our tackle boxes include Helin Flatfish in every size and color (especially frog, silver, gold, and black-orange), Rooster Tails, crankbaits, Rapalas, and other large spoons.

If you are without a downrigger, run a 3- or 4-foot line on the back hook of a deep countdown lure and tie on a Super Duper, a spinner, or a Rooster Tail. The added weight gets the lure down deeper and gives you an additional offering to the fish. If you are after bigger fish (you'll hardly feel a small fish if you do this), use a three-way swivel and tie a 1- or 2-ounce ball of lead to the bottom of the swivel on about a foot of line. Use only half the pound-test of your regular line—this way if you hang up, the lead will come off and you won't lose the lure. Then run your line back about six to twelve feet. Be careful of tangling your line with this rig.

If you can't get down to where the fish are, it's time to start jigging.

Knowing Your Life Jackets

Okay, the term *life jacket* is out of style these days—even though we all use it. You're supposed to call it a PFD (a personal flotation device). Give us a break—when was the last time you called it a PFD?

Since we've tipped a number of boats in our day, and spent some time floating and/or clinging to the upside-down boat (USDB) in the middle of the lake or river, it's nice to know we have quality and not one of those orange things.

Flotation devices are divided into five types:

• Type I is for offshore use;

• Type II and III are for near shore;

• Type IV is a square or ring-shaped flotation device for smooth, inland water with heavy traffic;

• Type V can be used for Type I, II, and III.

Any PFD certified for your intended use is fine as long as it fits the wearer correctly. Good PFDs also come in children's sizes and small sizes to fit women. Make sure you have a good life jacket for each person on board—and that each person wears it.

8

WHEN CONDITIONS AREN'T PERFECT
Challenging High Water and Winter Weather

Fishing may be as close to a perfect sport (or passion) as a human can find in this life. There's nothing like being on the water. However, conditions aren't always perfect. Sometimes the water isn't perfect. If you wait for a perfect day or the water to be just right, you're not going to get a lot of fishing in.

There are going to be times when things aren't as ideal as you'd hoped for. You can go home and turn on the TV and experience life vicariously; or, you can gut up and go fishing, improving your mind. You'll be a player, not one of those millions who lead a life of quiet desperation. In this chapter, we'll talk about several of the problems that discourage too many fisher-folk. And we'll tell you how to keep those problems from getting in the way of your fishing.

So just what do you do during the spring run-off, or when too much summer rain has made your favorite stream look like flowing coffee. You can sit and sulk, or you can learn how to fish high water. And what about cold weather? Do you hang up your rod during the

Foul-weather fishing

Fishing high water is a challenge.

winter? If you do, you're missing out on a lot of great, frosty fishing. Let's look at how to tease sullen fish into taking your lure.

HIGH WATER CONDITIONS

Be careful in high water. When that water gets high, you have to tread carefully. Both of us have taken aquatic tumbles. Fortunately, each time we were in small streams or one of us might not have been writing this book. Take every caution.

Locating and Presenting to the Fish

The water is the color of creamy, weak coffee. What do you do?

The single most important thing is to locate the fish. High-water conditions dangerously increase the volume of water, so it's nearly impossible to fish randomly. There's so much water to cover. If you don't know where the fish are, you aren't going to catch any.

Holding in the Deep Water. In raging torrents and in extreme high water, fish are likely to go deep. When the water gets high and flowing at a good clip, fish focus on finding gentle water, expending as few calories as possible, and not worrying about food unless it drifts right by their nose. Fish will hug the bottom in the deepest stretch of water, hold behind a rock to avoid the current, or hold next to the bank in the quiet water.

Nature has trained the fish to save energy in high water. In high water it's not a good strategy to go off chasing food. The calories expended may not be as great as the calories gained. The fish isn't going to move from its holding, nor will it patrol to find food. You'll have to find exactly where the fish is and cast to it. Moreover, you are going to have to drag your offering right past the fish's nose. It will move its head up, down, or to the side. Because it won't change depth, you'll want to be down far enough to feel your lure hit bottom from time to time.

If you don't know the water, it's tough. Look for slow-moving deep water. With a lure heavy enough to get down, systematically work the bottom until you find the fish. Retrieve just faster than the current. If you can safely wade

This water is unusually high for late November. Be careful because if you get wet, you're done for the day.

in the water, fish from below the hole. If the water is too tricky to get out into, inch out from the edge as far as you safely can.

Always use silver, bronze, or gold blades in these fishing situations. Lures like the heavier Panther Martins are effective since they have an excellent action. White and black tend to be our favorite colors.

The Edges. Don't ignore the gentler high water next to the bank. The edges are good during spring run-off when the water rises and is colored, but the flow isn't violent. At this time, a stable water level and an abundance of food provide for excellent feeding conditions.

Look for brushy banks, at least seven inches of water, and some sort of structure. Position yourself below the bank you want to fish (usually not a problem even in high water since you'll be close to the bank). Cast straight up or slightly to the edge. Begin retrieving just ahead of the current. If that doesn't produce fish, try a faster retrieve, moving the rod tip from side to side, which jiggles the lure. Now and then try completely stopping the action by not reeling for a moment or two.

Fish on the bank will be aggressive and aren't likely to be too frightened by the action of your lure. Fish in this water are feeding. They wouldn't be in these shallows if they weren't putting on the feed bag. As soon as they are full they will go back to hold in deep water.

In these situations, we like lures like Light Mepps and Rooster Tails that float across the water. These lures don't have to go deep.

Rising and Falling Water. You might be in for some good fishing in the summer after a heavy rain raises and discolors the water. An infusion of rain also cools and oxygenates the water as well as washes all sorts of insects, worms, and other goodies into the water.

Be aware, too, that as soon as the water crests and starts to recede, the fishing is so good many veteran anglers begin to salivate. During a fishing trip on the Logan, the water crested in the early morning so we came in and had breakfast while it peaked. By the time we got back on the stream, the water level had started to come down. On this day, we didn't bother trying to locate fish in the deep water; we fished the banks and cast to trout along the shoreline going after bugs.

Mucky and Yucky: Tips for Fishing Cloudy Water

We know of few anglers who enjoy high or cloudy water; however, there's no reason to go home. Get out there and catch some fish. Here are a few ideas:

- Fish can't see as well in cloudy water so they rely on their other senses. It will take a little longer for the fish to zone in on your offering. Slow down your retrieve so the steady rhythm of the lure's action will guide them to it.

- Some casters are unsure about where to search for fish in murky water. There are two good places to begin: 1) the shallow water right near the bank, or 2) next to structure (how deep will depend somewhat on the water temperature). Look for logs, snags, overhangs, rocks, moss lines, or shelves. Knowing this helps prevent spending all your time casting in the wrong water.

- In colored water, try spoons, rattle lures, and crankbaits. These lures are designed to send vibrations and make noise that attract fish.

COLD-WEATHER FISHING

When the snow starts to fly and the temperature freezes the cat's water solid, most spin casters hang up the rods, oil the reels, and dream of spring when the weather finally gets good again. That's too bad. Winter fishing can be a lot of fun. There's no reason to pack those rods and reels away for a winter nap when they can be poised for some exciting, if sometimes chilly, action.

While we agree winter fishing might not be as comfy as a spring jaunt, it's a whole lot better than sitting around the house watching poorly written fishing shows on TNN. After all, fishing (especially pursuing large specimens) is what we do. It is why we get up in the morning.

Every few casts you knock the ice off the rod guides and wonder what the heck you are doing freezing like this, and you'll be having the time of your life. You might wonder why you didn't add another layer of clothes or why you didn't bring another thermos of hot raspberry tea. . . . Well, any day you can fish, you have to thank God—winter be damned.

*One nice fish—
on ice!*

FISHING IN COLD WEATHER

While the concepts are the same, winter fishing has a slightly different twist. You have to cast by a slightly different set of rules even if you are on the same playing field. Let's take a look at the habits of the winter fish, where to locate our finned friends in freezing water, how to effectively cast to chill-water trout, and how to go into battle properly equipped.

The Habits of Winter Fish

"To know a winter fish is to love him (or her as the case might be)," Alan said to a group of young scouts one winter night. We were going to take them to the Provo River the next Saturday. To take it further, "to know a winter fish is to catch him."

Give or take a few degrees, a species of fish will have an optimum temperature where it feels most comfortable. A trout likes its water around 58 degrees. Ten degrees on either side of this, the fish will still be pretty comfortable. Beyond this, life starts to get uncomfortable and

the fish has to make adjustments. When the water gets colder, the fish slows down to cope with its environment.

With trout, for example, you'll notice that when the water gets below 47 degrees, things get pretty dull. When the water gets in the 30s, things really slow down. We've caught plenty of fish in cold water, but we've had to make adjustments.

The fish's heart rate is reduced, and its movements are more deliberate. It needs a lot less food to survive. It will hold in water that is deeper and slower, but with enough current to carry food to it.

In cold water, fish tend to pod up in comfortable areas. Most of the winter water you'll encounter will be fishless. Just because you caught fish there in the spring, summer, or fall doesn't mean you'll get into them come winter. It's critical that you focus on where the fish are (unless casting to keep yourself warm).

LETHARGIC FISH

Frostbite: Staying Out a Little Too Long

Frostbite, when skin and/or tissue actually freezes, is a lot like falling in love—it sneaks up on you when you're not expecting it. No one plans to be frostbit, but it happens to too many winter anglers. As you'd expect, your face, feet, and hands are at the greatest risk.

If the condition goes on too long, the tissue can be damaged or ruined. When seriously exposed, your body pumps more blood to the more important inner organs, and parts like your face, hands, and feet play a secondary role. Not only are they more likely to be exposed, they get less blood to warm them up.

By the way, sweat or moisture buildup on your skin makes matters worse. In fact, these areas are two or three times more likely to be frostbit than dry skin. It's easy to see how wet feet and wet hands—common conditions for casters—can be problematic.

There are different degrees of frostbite. A nip or frost nip is when the moisture in the skin freezes but the actual tissue doesn't freeze. This problem often affects the toes, the fingers, the nose, the cheeks, and the ears. If you catch this in time, it's a little painful but not serious. You can thaw the nipped areas if you warm them up. When you thaw out, the affected area usually feels burned (and can hurt like hell), you might get a few blisters, and the skin will typically look red. There are usually no lasting problems. Frostbite is really serious when the freeze goes deeper and destroys tissue.

Preventing Frostbite: Keep It Covered, Keep It Warm

There's no reason to stay home when it's cold. Rather, use some caution and dress accordingly. And, of course, use good judgment. There are a few things to remember.

- Dress in layers and don't move so much that you sweat. If you sweat, you're two or three times more at risk for hypothermia and frostbite. Stop and catch your breath more often. If you get warm, take off a layer or two—put it back on when you get cold. Remember that multiple layers trap air and are warmer than one layer.

- Drinking alcohol will actually chill you since it makes the blood lose heat. Smoking hinders your blood circulation and will cool you.

- A good hat, a good pair of gloves or mittens, and good-fitting footwear are critical parts of your outdoor wear. If your gloves or footwear are too tight, they will restrict the blood flowing to your hands or feet and you'll be cold.

If You're Frostbit: What Do You Do?

Of course the best advice is not to get bit in the first place, but if you do, what then? It's a serious problem all outdoor folk who brave cold weather need to consider. Michael, who gets cold a lot easier than Alan, has been frostbitten a number of times. One time it was dicey, but he still has all his fingers.

- Don't make it worse—seek warmth and shelter if any part of your body starts to feel numb! Do what you can to get out of the cold, get covered up, and get warm. If you can't get out of the cold, build a fire, get in a sleeping bag, drink something hot, or put on more clothing.

- Whenever possible, seek shelter before treating frostbite. Only treat it outdoors when you have no other choice. A frostbit limb that thaws, then is frostbit again, makes the situation worse.

- If your hands start to feel numb, tuck them in your groin area or under your arms. Cover up your head and put more on your feet.

- If your feet are affected, elevate them.

- Seek warmth, but don't get your affected area too close to artifical heat. Your body is numb and if you're not careful, you'll make the situation a whole lot worse by burning something. Michael has personal experience with this.

- As a frozen body part starts to warm up, it's best to move it a bit, though it will hurt like hell.

- Once back at the cabin, put the frostbit part in lukewarm water that feels slightly warm to your elbow if you dunk it in. It might take about a painful half-hour to thaw. If this doesn't help, better get serious medical help.

- Treat any blisters carefully with antiseptic cream.

Locating Fish in Freezing Water

Find the Comfort Zone. Focus on the slow, deep-water pools in which fish can conserve calories, but where current drifts some food to them.

Also look for warmer water—even a few degrees up the mercury. If you can find them, underground springs and seeps are the best places to start. This water will be a constant temperature year-round, warmer than the normal winter flow, and will support more aquatic insects. Fish will pack into these places like cordwood. The trick is finding such waters. One of the best ways is to ask around. Another way is to scout for springs and seeps in the summer when the water is low.

Spring Creeks. Spring creek water comes out of the earth or mountainside. This water has a constant temperature and for a while, at least, will have a warmer temperature than normal water that has been already buffeted by the cold winter weather and freezing rain and snow. Fish will congregate in these pockets and fishing can be very good.

Tailwater. A tailwater is water that comes out of the bottom of a dam, creating artificial spring creek conditions. As a result, the water has a constant temperature. Tailwaters are excellent fishing. Some of the best four-star, blue-ribbon trout streams in this country are tailwaters: the San Juan River, the Green River, and the White River, among others.

Cold-Water Casting Tricks

Casting Up and Back. Stand in the stream below or to the side of where you think the fish are holding. Cast up and ahead of the fish, giving your lure enough time to get on the bottom. Once it is deep enough, reel it just faster than the current, trying all the while to keep it as deep as you can.

If you reel in too fast, you'll scare the fish. You want your lure to have some action. Because a smaller lure is critical, we often use $1/32$- and $1/8$-ounce spinners, and occasionally a $1/7$-ounce spinner. Tiny hardware won't be as likely to spook the fish, is easier to control, and is not as likely to hang up (and when it does, it's easier to undo). Be aware, too, that hanging up on the bottom is a part of this process.

Minnows and Banks. If you get a warm snap in the winter that lasts a couple of days, don't overlook the banks. This weather change can heat up a very shallow, flat section of water. Besides bringing on a hatch, the relative warmth sometimes makes small minnows real active in these areas, which attracts larger fish. Use small, shiny lures. Silver Kastmasters and Super Dupers are our favorites in such conditions.

You'll want to cast from a distance because the fish will be very spooky in such water. Cast your spinner and let it flash as you reel it in slowly.

Vertical "Stream" Jigging. Sometimes you'll encounter deep pools that are hard to fish. If there is a sharp drop-off, you can borrow techniques used by jigging lake casters. If the water is deep, possibly a little cloudy, and not dangerously high, you can stand close to the edge. If the water is deep enough and big enough for a small boat like a canoe or a float tube, so much the better.

Because the trick is to get right over where the fish are holding, a long rod comes in handy when stream fishing. You can reach over to the lie and drop your lure much easier.

Fish are going to be slow and possibly easily frightened. Use a small, flashy lure. Let small sections of line out until the lure hits the bottom. Remember to be ready because the flutter of the lure on the way down can attract a fish. Once the lure hits the bottom, lift it slightly and let it flutter back down. Lift and flutter. Keep repeating the action. Remember, slow and easy. What you're trying to do is create an interesting action to motivate a lethargic fish to come over and look at it.

Earlier we suggested that, generally, dragging a lure through stream water once is often enough—if a fish is interested it'll take it. Winter fishing is an exception. You have to tempt the fish repeatedly, especially when jigging and spinning a hole. You need to be patient in this game of cat and mouse.

If a lift and flutter doesn't work, modify your technique. Let your hardware hit the bottom. Take up the slack and reel the line in a few inches. Lift the lure up a few inches and let it drop by lowering the rod tip. Continue to do this. Reel up another seven or eight inches and let it drop. Experiment by moving the rod tip from side to side. Continue to reel until you are a foot or two off the bottom. Check your lure and start again. Frequently, the fish will hit the lure when it is dropping, not on the lift.

Some pools are easier to work by standing above them. The down and across is a favorite technique when this is the case—and is good on fish anytime of the year. Stand above the pool you want to fish, far enough up so you don't spook the fish. Locate where you think the best fish lie is—the place you want to work your lure.

If the current isn't strong enough to hold your lure fluttering, retrieve just fast enough upstream to keep your lure from hanging up. After a few simple casts, use the rod tip to drag the lure from side to side as you retrieve, varying the movement. Carefully work the water, giving your hardware enough time to get on the bottom before you bring it in. You'll have to experiment with this method, but it can be very effective. Be sure to work the lure as slowly as you can.

If the water has enough current to flutter your lure without you actively retrieving it, try this. Let the line out in the current or cast. Let the lure drop above the lie. Impart a "more alive" motion by keeping the line taut and pulling the tip up slightly. After you've worked the lure in this position, let it swing to either the right or left in the current. Keeping the hardware positioned in the water gives the fish a chance to come and investigate. Remember, it's not going to move too fast, so you have to hold it. Work the water carefully and keep the lure as close to the bottom as you can. We've preached small lures, and we still hold to that, but this is one case where it might be better to go a little heavier if it means keeping your lure in front of the fish's nose.

Also try casting to one of the sides of the pool. Let the hardware swing in the current and retrieve. This motion is very tempting. Keep it low and slow!

COLD-WEATHER GEAR

Getting cold is not a laughing matter. Hypothermia claims more lives than a hundred years of rattlesnake bites.

Hat. Remember your mother telling you to put on a hat if your feet are cold—or something like that? In cold weather, a hat is a necessity. We won't go into much detail on hats, other than they need to be warm and protect your ears. Hats also need to be windproof unless you have a hooded parka. If your ears are really sensitive, wear an ear band under your hat. We've had great luck with wool and fleece.

Keep Your Hands Warm. If anything is going to get wet and cold, it's going to be your hands. Releasing fish doesn't keep you dry. A soft-

Dress in layers in cold weather. Jon-Michael is wearing thick long johns, fleece, and several pairs of socks.

basket net is a great help. It's easy to release the fish and keep your fingers out of the water.

Gloves or mittens are a must. Since your gloves might get wet, carry a second pair as a back up. We carry a second pair of mittens. You might not feel comfortable fishing in them, but you'll need them to warm you up. Most of the time, we fish in fingerless wool gloves, which do not restrict dexterity and do allow us to tie on spinners. Michael's have a top that flops over the fingers when he doesn't need dexterity. Wool is a good fabric choice because it still has some insulating value if you get wet. On really cold days we carry little hand and foot warmers we can fire up if our fingers or toes get numb. You can find these handy packets at most ski and outdoor shops.

Layers. Dress in layers so you can add or take off clothes as the conditions demand. Down vests, heavy shirts, wool sweaters, and fleece are great for warm layering. The final layer should be windproof and waterproof. For underwear you'll want some sort of a polypropylene that wicks moisture, then perhaps a heavier long john followed by wool or fleece pants. Use cotton as a last choice since it holds moisture.

Coat or Parka. It gets really cold if you're sitting in a boat all day and not moving. A nice heavy coat to go over your layers is always smart. It stands to reason that your outer garment should be large enough to comfortably fit over your layers. If you don't have a good coat, add more layers and make sure your outer garment is windproof.

Socks. Like your other clothes, you should layer socks as well. The first sock should be poly, unless you have a sock with a poly layer in it. Wool blends are best. Never, never, never, never, never wear cotton if it's cold. A too-tight fit will cut off your circulation and you'll get cold even if you have three pairs on.

Wading Belts. Most chest waders have belts. In summer the belts make waders warmer than you might like, but in winter, you'll welcome the extra warmth. At any time of year, they'll help keep the water out if you take a tumble.

Hypothermia: The Least You Should Know

What you know about hypothermia can save you. What you don't know can kill you. People die from hypothermia. In case you missed that, let us say it again. People die from hypothermia—and it ain't all that uncommon.

Hypothermia occurs when a person's body temperature drops and they get seriously cold. When body temperature drops below 98 degrees, the victim starts to shiver—the body's way of warming up. When body temperature drops to about 94 degrees, the victim will shiver radically.

After 89 degrees, shivering stops and the person loses dexterity and moves as if drunk. A person will pass out if the temperature drops to 84 degrees and will die if the temperature drops into the 70s.

Hypothermia rarely occurs above an air temperature of 65 degrees. Most cases occur between freezing and 55 degrees.

A person is more susceptible to hypothermia if wet. Heat will leave your body about twenty-five times faster if your clothes are wet than if your clothes are dry. Wind is also a killer. This is why seeking shelter is so important. For example, at an air temperature of 40 degrees a ten-mile-per-hour wind will have a wind-chill factor of 30 degrees; a twenty-mile-per-hour wind, 20 degrees; and a thirty-mile-per-hour wind, 10 degrees.

Food and Drink. Okay, we're all on diets, but don't worry about your weight when you are winter fishing. Eat all the junk you want. It helps keep you warm. Keep a pocket full of candy bars and bags of nuts and munch away. Have a greasy hamburger before you hit the water. All that fat will keep you warm. Also carry a thermos of something hot and take periodic drinks.

Waders. If the weather is cold, you need thick waders. Neoprene waders five millimeters thick are best. If you have another type, perhaps the thin, comfortable variety, you'll need to layer up a lot more.

Be Careful. There's a time to go back to the vehicle and head home. Use good judgment. Live to fish another day.

9
CATCH AND RELEASE
Handle with Care

Michael tells of the time he and his son Jon-Michael went to Yellowstone Park on June 15 for the opening day of cutthroat fishing on Yellowstone Lake. This is almost a religious holiday for the Rutters, Michael being a devotee of this lovely fish—especially the Yellowstone species. He's passed "cutt fever" on to his children.

After several days of glorious casting, they begrudgingly left cutthroat nirvana and drove north to meet Alan for some pike fishing in Canada. On their way home, after several weeks of fishing, they stopped in the park once again for more cutt action. Mike insisted and Jon-Michael seconded the motion.

They noticed there were occasional dead trout washed up on the shore. With some exceptions, the park is basically catch and release. It didn't take a rocket scientist to figure out the problem. Most, if not all, the dead cutts washed

Jim Dunlevy releases a fine steelhead back into the Rogue River in southern Oregon. Michael fought this fish for over twenty minutes.

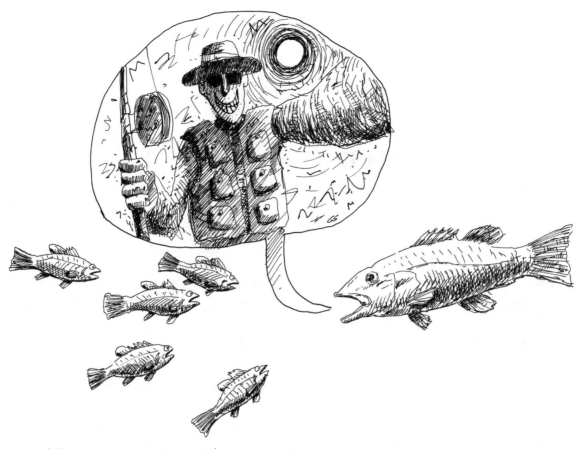

THE OLDEST FISH IN THE LAKE TELLS HIS TALE
OF ALIEN ABDUCTION TO THE SMALL FRY.

up on the shoreline were the victims of bad catch-and-release techniques—what we sadly call "catch and die later, damnit" thanks to ignorant casters' poor handling.

A fish is a valuable resource and can be hooked again and again if done right. A fish hasn't got a prayer if it isn't released properly. The truth is the old boy who goes out with wicked wads of PowerBait and catches his limit and goes home may be killing far fewer fish than the person catching and releasing poorly. Why? He catches and keeps his limit and goes home for a fish fry. The person who poorly releases a lot of fish is likely killing a lot more than the "die and fry" man with bait.

Here's how you can avoid becoming a killer of innocent fish:

1. Reel the fish in quickly—fight it no longer than necessary. Avoid stressing the fish. If a fish reaches a certain stress level by being played to exhaustion, chemical changes take place in its anatomy, which too often equal a blindfold and last cigarette. Release it as quickly as you can.

2. Wet your hands before touching the fish. A fish has a slime or mucus that protects the fish against infection. If you touch a fish with dry hands, you'll remove some of the slime and possibly expose the fish to infection. This slime also helps reduce the friction between water and skin by acting as a lubricant. Any time you rub this protective, lubricating mucus off, you reduce the fish's chance of survival. If you use a net, use a high-grade cotton basket—never use nylon.

3. Don't grab the fish too tightly or touch the gill area. Because water lifts and upholds, fish bones and connective tissues aren't as

strong as those of creatures on the land. This is why you need to hold a fish gently when you pick it up to release the hook—or better yet, keep it in the water when you unhook the hook. Fish wiggle like mad to get away, and there's a temptation to grip hard—don't! Hold the fish firmly while you get the hook—but don't hold too firmly. Don't touch the eyes or the gills. If you finger the gills, or see blood in the gill area, it's almost certain the fish won't make it. Some anglers feel holding the fish upside down helps keep it from wiggling—try it and see. We're still not sure.

4. Keep the fish in the water as long as you can. Don't lift the fish out of the water if you don't have to. Try to release a fish while it's still in the drink. Often you can hold the fish and hold the hook—releasing in one fluid motion. Specially designed hook removers are available at most good fishing shops, but a hemostat or pliers will do the trick if used judiciously.

5. Cut the leader if the hook is embedded too deeply. You may have to sacrifice a lure or the hook. If the lure is deep, near the gills, or too difficult to get out, cut the leader or the hook ring. If the lure is small, you can cut the line. If the hook is large, cut the shaft of the hook "hook ring." Obviously you'll need to carry pliers or a Leatherman that will cut a hook shaft or a ring. Don't be afraid to leave a hook in a fish's mouth. It will dissolve in no time. You risk more damage handling a fish too long or too hard while trying to get the hook out. Pinch down the barbs on your hooks to make removal easier—or replace a treble hook with a single hook.

6. Support the fish in the water after you've released it until it swims off under its own power. No matter how carefully you try to get the fish in fast (and the hook out quickly), there will be times when the fish is almost too tired to take off on his own. If you let it wobble off unsupported, it will turn belly up. Let the fish rest and catch its breath. Hold it gently under its belly and under the tail—suspending it in the water. In a moment, it will zip off to a favorite hiding spot—thanking you for your kindness after slamming a hook through its upper jaw.

A soft cotton net is easier on the fish.

7. Give the fish artificial respiration if necessary. We're not talking about mouth to mouth—but at times you will have to resuscitate a fish if it's too exhausted to swim off. This is necessary if, when you are supporting the fish, it can't stay right side up on its own. The fish, then, is literally starving for oxygen. Run some water through the gill plates and get this fish breathing. If you're in a stream, face the fish up current. Gently move it back and forth so the gills absorb oxygen. Keep going until the fish can move its gills on its own.

Gently support a worn-out fish in the current, letting water run through its gills. Here Alan releases a fine brown back into the Green River.

If possible, keep the fish in the water while you release the hook. Handle the fish gently.

Handle 'Em with Care

TACKLE
- Use barbless hooks or pinch the barbs down with pliers.
- Use heavier line so you can bring your fish in more quickly.
- Don't use overly large hooks. Big hooks, especially if the fish isn't very large, can damage the eyes or parts of the mouth.
- Don't touch the gills.

LANDING YOUR FISH
- Bring your fish in quickly.
- Keep the fish in the water for the entire experience if possible; if you have to bring it out of the water, do so as quickly as you can.
- Have your camera set up before the fish is ready to release. (Easier said than done, but it's possible). No excess fumbling. Call someone over to take the picture.
- If you can, avoid using a cheap net, which can sometimes damage a fish's skin.
- Don't squeeze the fish.

GETTING THE HOOK OUT
- If you can, get the hook out while the fish is in the water.
- Use needle-nose pliers or a hemostat to take the hook out.
- If the hook is set in deep, don't try to get it out; cut the line.

REVIVING YOUR FISH
- Point your fish's nose into the current and gently move it back and forth; its gills need to be working on their own.
- If the fish wants to go, let it go.
- If you catch a trophy fish, and you have a really tough battle, you may have to work a moment to revive it.

HAVE YOUR CAMERA READY.

To Kill or Not to Kill Your Catch

If you're going to kill some fish to eat, that's your decision. We hope you'll mostly take planted fish and spare the natives. We advocate catch-and-release fishing and practice it fairly religiously. Nevertheless, we're not above a good fish dinner. Fish are good eating.

In a park fished as heavily as Yellowstone, for example, catch and release is the only way to go. Because some joker dumped lake trout in Yellowstone Lake, native cutthroat are threatened and every one should be released.

There are some fanatics that say you should never kill a fish. We say to use good sense and sound management judgment. In a place like a national park where there's a lot of pressure, taking fish is a foolish thing. The resource can't handle it. But in blue-ribbon or trophy waters, especially where the fish grow slowly, we tend to keep the midsize fish for eating, letting the bigger and smaller fish go.

If you hook into a trophy, congratulations! Take a few photos while you carefully measure the length and girth of the catch. Then release it. Why deny some other angler the thrill you just experienced? Monster fish should live to be caught again. If you're desperate to have the fish on your wall, take the measurements and photos of the beast to a taxidermist who specializes in trophy recreations (the fake ones often look more lifelike than the stuffed real ones).

When you take some fish, consider the following to ensure a tasty meal. Fish go bad quickly if not handled properly. Kill the fish right away—a stressed fish produces chemical changes that affect the meat's flavor. Wack the fish on the back of the head or snap the neck. Cut or break out the gills to allow the fish to bleed. Clean your fish as soon as you can—get those guts out. If you're handy with a fillet knife, like Alan, that's a great way to go.

Put the fish on ice (not touching one another if possible) or store on a stringer in the water (never put live fish on a stringer). And lastly, don't put your catch in plastic bags. Doing so will taint the flavor. Eat well! Someday, Alan will write a book on cooking fish—he's the best.

10
LANDING TROPHY FISH
Banking and Boating Fish That Could Bust Your Line

When you pray at night, pray for a fish to strain your line. Then hope you're worthy of the challenge. Catching trophy fish, fish that can easily break your line if you aren't careful, is the reason we get up in the morning.

When you do hook into a good fish, you want to land it. You don't want it to bust off. Inevitably, no matter how good you are, you'll lose some fish. That's why they call it fishing, not catching. However, what we want to do in this chapter is raise the odds a bit.

Most of us don't catch many really big fish; thus we don't tax our tackle. And since we don't catch a lot of monsters, we don't get that much practice with the real rod benders. If you play a large fish like you do a small fish, all you'll have is a curled wad of mono, a lost lure, and a sworn blue streak. Nevertheless, half the sport of taking trophy fish is taking them on light line—line that can break if you aren't careful.

Michael is our resident lake trout man. He's landed several fish over forty pounds with

Michael caught this lunker rainbow after a late-spring snowstorm. It took nearly an hour to bring the fish in.

YOU'VE GOT TO <u>THINK</u> TO OUTSMART THE FISH.

4-pound-test line. It's a giant game of chess, you against the fish. It takes practice, but it can be done. Alan is the bucketmouth man (in more ways than one), and he enjoys jigging for bucketmouth with light line. This is quite a feat when you remember how much structure there is to get hung up on in most bass waters. What we're saying is we've lost a few fish, but we've landed our fair share also.

So What Is a Trophy Fish?

For our purposes here, let's assume it's a fish that taxes your fishing tackle—a fish that could break off if you aren't careful how you handle it.

The water you are fishing is another factor to consider. Alan has taken to catching largemouth bass on 2- to 4-pound-test. Because of the shape of the fish and the never-ending structure that increases the risk of a break off, Alan's seven-pound bass on 2-pound-test line is quite a trophy. More so, perhaps, than the forty-two-pound lake trout Mike caught on 4-pound-test line.

Tips for Turning a Running Fish

If you've hooked a valiant fish and it runs downstream, you'll need to turn it into the current. When a fish gets into the drift, the flow more than doubles the strength of the fish, straining your line. You've got to try to get its nose pointed upstream. However, turning a fish is easier said than done.

Sometimes changing the angle of the line will reverse the run. Consider the following tips that work about half the time:

The Ol' Rod Tip in the Water Trick

- Stick your rod tip in the water.

- Administer pressure, keeping plenty of tension on without breaking the line (if the water is deep, push the rod tip deeper). Make sure your drag is set correctly.

- This will reverse the pressure on the line. This modification in line tension sometimes causes the fish to reverse directions and go upstream.

The Ol' Pumping the Rod Trick

- Very smartly, but not with so much force you strain the line, try long radical pumps, dropping the rod tip and then raising it again.

- Changing the pressure on the line can make the fish turn.

When fighting a large fish, sometimes it helps to lower the rod, keep reeling, and pull to the side.

To keep a fish off balance, pump the rod—drop the rod while you reel, then lift it again. Always keep the line snug.

HANDLING DEEP-WATER FISH

If you plan to release deep-water fish after you've hooked them, don't bring them up too fast. Pay close attention to lake trout and walleye—or any fish you hook deeper than thirty feet.

Bringing a fish up too fast can enlarge its bladder or burst the stomach and other organs. Many lakers, walleyes, and stripers swim to their deaths after being lovingly released by well-meaning anglers who've brought the fish up too fast.

Keep the pressure on such a fish when you hook it, but don't bring it up too fast. Enjoy the fight, and bring it up slowly.

AVOIDING COMMON MISTAKES

When you are trying to land a large fish, you have to walk a fine line (pun intended).

If you horse the fish, the lunker could snap the line. At the same time, if you're too wimpy, Moby Dick will run away with the line—then snap it.

You have to finesse in a fish—especially a large one if your tackle is light. It's a game of chess, you against a water bullet with fins. You have to put enough positive pressure on the fish to keep it under control, but not so much you break your line. Your goal is to take in the line and bring the fish toward you. The fish takes a few feet; you try to get it back.

We've talked generally about landing that big one, but now let's look at some specifics. We'll assume that your gear is in good shape, especially your line. Remember, your line is your connection with the fish. When you have a twenty-pound steelhead hen on 8-pound-test line and she's turned into the main current of the Rogue River, your line will have a lot of stress on it. It has to be in perfect condition. Any imperfection will weaken your line and you'll risk losing your fish.

Now what do you do to keep that fish under control? Let's take a trip through the Rutter-Baumgarten how-to-keep-the-damn-fish-hooked tips we've learned by trial and error. This stuff comes from sad experience. We've lost a lot of really nice fish. When we talk about the ones that got away we can make a pretty

Always net larger fish headfirst. If you don't, you run a good risk of losing your fish.

Be sure to tire the fish out before netting it.

long list. As a result of our, shall we say, losses, we've made a study of how to do it right.

Keep a Close Eye on the Drag. Your drag is a major part of your fish-fighting gear. A good drag is critical for big fish. A big fish tugging against a drag wears out a reel fast. Ever notice how some reels are listed for $30 and some for $100. A major reason is the drag system. Adjust it before you fish and every so often to double-check. Don't cinch it tight "so I can really set the hook." Set the drag so you can pull line without breaking it, and then back it off just a little more. Alan once lost an enormous largemouth at Lake Powell because he forgot to adjust the drag after switching to a lighter line. The monster struck, jumped once to show off, and then vanished with a Rapala in its great maw.

Leave the drag set. If you snag up, don't tighten up the drag to break off. Not only will this wear out your drag, sooner or later you'll forget to reset it. Instead, hold the spool until the line breaks. By the same consideration, if you need more line, don't pull out line against the drag. Open up the bail.

Rip Out Their Lips, Baby! Sometimes a fish just naturally sets the hook (especially if you are trolling), but you never have any way of being sure. That's why you have to get in the habit of setting the hook solidly when you get a strike.

Some fish, bass and lake trout for example, have hard, bony mouths. You have to set that hook hard, even on midsize models. Most trophy-size fish of any species will have a hard mouth.

When you feel the fish strike, slam that rod tip up. Envision the hook being jerked through that pouting fish lip.

Rod Tips Up, Baby! Keep that dang tip up when you hook a lunker, but don't hold it too high. This makes the fish argue with the flex in your rod and you avoid putting too much strain on your line.

If you're holding the rod butt near your waist line, the tip should be about chest high. If you're holding your rod butt near your chest, your tip should be about head high. This way your rod can do its job and you can keep your line snug. You can also move your rod to either side to adjust pressure on the fish.

Tip up, however, doesn't mean over your head! If your rod is up too high, it will lose some of its shock-absorbing qualities. We might add that this is how a lot of rods are broken. Of course you'll have superior bragging rights, but you'll still have to buy a new rod.

Reeling in the Fish. There are several things to remember. Don't reel in on a running fish. Reel down to the fish as you lower the rod tip. Remember that your rod tip is up. After you've been exerting positive pressure, drop your rod tip toward the water, reeling like a mad person while you do so. This is called reeling to the fish. Then, with your rod tip pointed toward the water, lift the rod tip, bringing in the fish and gaining line, until it runs again. Obviously the strength of the line will have a lot to do with how much you lift. This will wear the fish out and bring it closer to you.

Keep Up the Pressure. Maintain positive pressure and don't give up any line you don't have to. Move the rod tip from side to side to pressure the fish from different angles.

There is one exception. If you are fighting a really big fish in close and it jumps, drop your rod toward the fish to ease the tension. It's a tough call.

Respect a Green Fish. A green fish is a fish that isn't tired, yet. It is still strong and will take a lot of runs. Your job is to keep it in check and keep as much line as possible on your spool. Let the fish run but keep the pressure on. What you want to do is tire the fish. A lot of good fish are lost at this stage of the game. Anglers get so eager to land the trophy, they horse too much or they tighten up the drag. Along these same lines, don't try to get the fish in too close before it's tired. Often, even a large fish will let you reel it in close. After it sees you, it will make its first major run. Also, there's a better chance that it will tangle the line or run under the boat. If the fish gets in too tight, angle your rod to absorb the shock of the fish. Many experienced anglers don't try to get the fish in close. They want it a ways out before it runs.

Lighten Up as the Fish Gets in Close. Remember, when you get your trophy in close, you'll need to lighten up the pressure. Your line is shorter and you don't have as much stretch in your line as you did with more line out. You'll need to bring the fish in carefully. Don't horse it at the last minute. When you have a fish with 30 yards of line out, give it hell. Fight it hard. If you have a fish with 3 yards of line out, go easy.

Mess with the Fish's Head. Move the rod from side to side as you are fighting the fish to keep the fish off balance.

Netting the Catch. A lot of fish are lost at netting. Remember to tire out a fish before you try and get a net under it. Also remember that when you shove that net in the water, it's going to spook the fish. Net the fish headfirst. The theory is the fish will swim into the net. If you net it tail first, it will spook and run.

11

ALPINE ANGLING
Great Fishing Where Summer Barely Comes

The high country has a majesty all its own. Summer is short and cool, and winter is cold, long, and lingering. The air is thin and crisp, and snow is a possibility even in July and August. And while the air might be thin, nothing tastes better to breathe.

An alpine lake might be little more than a pond you could throw a stone across—or a body of water thirty acres or more. As a rule, most lakes aren't large.

The result of down-reaching glaciers gouging out the soil and rocks, alpine lakes are literally fishing jewels nestled among some of the finest peaks on God's green earth–and arguably some of the best fishing water you're likely to find. While you can drive to a few high-mountain waters, most alpine lakes require some walking (or the services of a trusty hay burner). The problem, or maybe it's not a problem, is getting there. Leg power is the standard

If you don't mind burning a little shoe leather, a wonderful world of fishing awaits you.

method, so less fishing pressure is the order of the day.

Since the water is clear and pure (which can't help but have a cleansing effect upon you), the fish are bright and colorful. The harsh winters and cool water produce a fish that is strong and bold, as well as good to eat. The flesh is usually salmon pink since crustaceans are the major food source. Such fish, fried or foiled over coals, is a treat fit for the gods.

At times, high lakes are some of the fastest fishing you'll ever encounter. As a caster you can't do anything wrong—whatever you're offering is taken by eager trout that all but thank you as you reel them in. At other times, you'll see fish all over the place and nothing you can do will tempt them. It can be the most frustrating experience in the world—dozens of fish popping up all over and you get *nada*.

You can wait the fish moods out (fish moods sometimes change fast on mountain lakes).

Perhaps you could move to another lake—maybe over the next rise. It's not unusual for one lake to be as dead as an old battery while another water five hundred yards away has fish lined up for you to catch. It's uncertain business at best.

The other alternative is to learn a little more about the nature of mountain lakes and do a lot more fish fighting than casting.

NATURE OF AN ALPINE LAKE

Many alpine lakes are filled with wonderful fish, but not all. Some lakes are fishless. It won't do you any good to cast in a fishless lake. Not long ago, we were sampling the alpine fishing in southern Oregon. We were a fair hike in from the Blue Rock trailhead when we came upon several frustrated anglers. They had a nice camp set up in front of a very pretty, small lake.

"How's fishing?" we asked.

"Pretty rotten," the couple replied almost at the same time.

"It's pretty maddening," the man said, "we've worked about the water and tried every lure in my tackle box."

Frequently, the only way to get to untapped lakes is to backpack in.

Fish will hold near structure. Fallen logs on alpine lakes make excellent places to cast.

High-Alpine Species

Cutthroat Trout. Cutts do well at high altitude, primarily in the western United States. Cutts like colder water and lots of structure. In the Rocky Mountain West, some strains of this fish are indigenous.

Cutts may not be the smartest trout, if any trout is smart, and anglers consider them the easiest to catch. They seem to like bronze spinners (the Super Duper #503, Jake's Spin-a-Lure, and white Rooster Tails are always in our tackle box). Cutts will come up out of nowhere and take your offering, fighting like gut-shot grizzlies.

Rainbow Trout. 'Bows are a favorite with fish management and are often stocked, especially in lower lakes. They are a hardy transplant but don't do as well as cutts at high altitude. Rainbows require a little deeper water than the cutts and are less likely to be in the shallows. 'Bows and cutts are cousins, by the way. If they are in the same water at lower altitudes, they will mix, making a "cutbow." Usually the rainbow's genetics will win out.

Brook Trout. You can find the brookie in many alpine lakes, usually at lower altitudes. They breed like rabbits and can stunt if they aren't fished out.

Most brookies are under a foot long and fight hard for their size. This eastern drainage fish was transplanted to the Rockies and the West and has done quite well. We rarely feel bad about taking a mess of brookies to the fire, leaving the cutts to grow some more.

Arctic Grayling. The grayling is a very interesting fish, and perhaps the easiest fish on this list to catch—most of the time. They will take anything. Grayling put up a great fight, but when they feel the battle is hopeless, they give up and are reeled in without ceremony.

Most alpine grayling are transplants. In many areas, fishing for them is catch and release only. They have a wonderfully tall fin and a very tiny mouth. For best results, fish a small spinner.

Lake Trout. Lakers haunt the deeper waters of the larger, deeper lakes, but come into the shallows to feed on small fish. They are great sport and wonderful table fare. After ice-out or in late fall, the laker will hold in shallower water. Spoons and bigger spinners aren't necessary, but they do help to get your presentation near the bottom. It's best to get your lure as deep as you can.

Don't Fish Dead Water. The couple could have fished there until they turned one hundred and two. There weren't fish in that water. This seems silly, but we see it all too often in the backcountry. Not every patch of water holds fish. It pays to do a little investigating. Check local or regional bookstores for fishing guidebooks on the area or ask the local Forest Service, fish and wildlife department, or hiking clubs.

Otherwise, you can use your eyes and investigate the lake. There has to be some depth to the water. A shallow body of water will freeze completely in the winter and kill the fish. The water in question has to be deep enough for the fish to ride out the winter. Take a few minutes, sit down, and watch the lake. See if you can see fish working the surface. Look for splashes or rings. Look closely at the shallows for cruising fish (this is easier if you can climb up a bank).

A good percentage of lakes have at one time or another been planted with fish—sometimes by plane, sometimes by donkey. Fish are native in other drainage systems.

If we could hazard a generalization, most lakes aren't too large, maybe three to five acres. And not all lakes, even though they have fish, have equally good fishing. Some lakes simply produce more fish than others, and some lakes at different times, for a number of reasons, are hotter or colder than other lakes—even lakes a stone's throw away. It sometimes takes a little fishing trial and error, which is part of the fun. Don't be afraid to do some lake hopping.

On the southern Oregon backpacking trip where we met the folks fishing the dead water, this concept was very obvious. Take Mud Lake for example. On the way in, a week earlier, it was as hot as a coke oven. On the way out, it was as cold as an Eskimo Pie. We knew there were fish; we had caught them.

Characteristics of Alpine Waters

Lake bottoms are often littered with boulders left over from glaciers that have gouged out bowls in the valley. The melting ice created lakes composed of a deep section (the cirque) and a flatter part (the moraine).

Boulders and/or fallen logs constitute the large portion of structure. These lakes aren't fertile by "low-lake" standards, but good populations of fish can live in this fairly harsh environment. As you'd suppose, these lakes are covered with ice a good part of the year, so during the summer months fish try to make up for lost time by indulging in feeding frenzies.

Depending on where you go, you might encounter some lakes that get little to no fishing pressure. While high lakes are wonderfully beautiful, they can also be quite fickle, as we've suggested. There are frustrating times when a lake will suddenly go dead after a period when anything you threw at the fish drew strikes.

All waters, especially mountain lakes, have good windows of fishing opportunity, usually in the mornings and evenings when fish are easy to catch and will take whatever you throw at them. There are also times when everything goes dead as a graveyard. Thank goodness the moods on these extraordinary lakes change quickly—and that another lake is just down the trail.

What to Throw and Why

When in doubt, go small.

For several reasons, most of your lures should be on the smaller side. First, larger lures

A mountain lake at ten thousand feet. Where would you make your first cast?

Once you head down the trail, you can't run back to the car for an extra lure or a candy bar. Plan carefully.

A small Mepps, a Rooster Tail, a small Panther Martin, and the never-fail Jake's Spin-a-Lure should be in every alpine tackle box.

have a tendency to scare all but the most aggressive fish. Second, and perhaps more important, alpine fish mainly eat tiny food.

For the most part, a high-country fish eats nymphs, scuds (a type of freshwater shrimp), and other insects (terrestrials). While this is primarily a spincasting book, most successful alpine casters have a few backup flies and a couple of bubbles (clear bobbers, sometimes called floats). When there's a lot of top-water action, a fly on a bubble can be deadly.

We'd recommend these flies for your spinning box: a few colors and sizes of the woolly bugger (#8–14); hopper patterns (#10–14); ant patterns (#12–18); Adams (#14–18), this may be one of the best all around flies; royal coachman (#14–18); and mosquito (#16–18).

You should have a general selection of $\frac{1}{32}$-, $\frac{1}{8}$-, and $\frac{1}{4}$-ounce lures. Perhaps your greatest selection should be in the $\frac{1}{4}$- to $\frac{1}{8}$-ounce area. If you plan to fish for lake trout, take along a supply of $\frac{1}{2}$-ounce lures so you can cast far and get down deep. Our boxes would not be complete without the following:

- A variety of Mepps spinners ($\frac{1}{8}$, $\frac{1}{4}$ ounce)

- Super Duper #503 in silver and bronze

- Jake's Spin-a-Lure, bronze and silver

- Panther Martins ($\frac{1}{32}$, $\frac{1}{8}$, $\frac{1}{4}$ ounce)

- Rooster Tails (all sizes, mostly whites, great for cutts)

Other Favorites

- Small spoons, Dardevles (red-white, yellow)

- Kastmasters ($\frac{1}{8}$ ounce, $\frac{1}{4}$ ounce, silver, and bronze)

- Krocodiles (different sizes and colors)

- Z-Rays (different sizes and colors)

- A small selection of jigs (white, black, red)

- Flies

- Ball-bearing swivels

12
WILD TROUT
Siren of the Wilderness

There are more than one hundred species or subspecies of trout in the world. It's surprising how many anglers go through their fishing lives in blissful trout ignorance. The more you learn about the fish you pursue, the more fish you'll catch—it's just like magic. So, let's take a few minutes to discuss the species trout.

BROWN TROUT (*SALMO TRUTTA*)

A brown is like no other trout.

It's a joy in and of itself, and it's probably Alan's favorite fish (though he has a hard time admitting it). When you set the hook (usually after a delicate pickup), you've hooked into some heavy-duty aquatic horsepower. The brown is a strong fighter with a muscular front and the determination to confront you until all its strength is drained. It's rarely a jumper like

a 'bow. The brown heads for the bottom of the pool or the deepest water, into the roughest line-breaking cover.

There's a cult of dedicated brown trout anglers (Alan and Michael are lifetime members). Brown trout have ruined love lives (ask Alan), broken marriages (ask Alan), delayed college degrees (ask Alan), broken mother's hearts (ask Alan).

The brown has turned out to be a somewhat cosmopolitan sort, a world traveler, by any fish's standards. Originally, this fish haunted the waters of North Africa (Algeria and Morocco), most of Europe, the Mediterranean area, Siberia, the Arctic, the Black Sea drainage, Asia, and Great Britain.

It is the dandy of the fly caster and spin caster alike and arguably the most difficult trout to hook. As a point of interest, many anglers, including the snootiest blue-blooded British fly

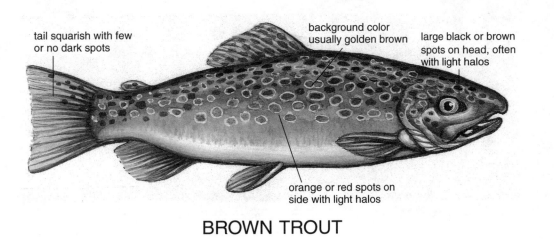

tail squarish with few or no dark spots

background color usually golden brown

large black or brown spots on head, often with light halos

orange or red spots on side with light halos

BROWN TROUT

casters, refer to the brown as *the* trout. Pound for pound, all else being equal (water temperature, food, and such), the brown will give you the greatest battle. We've logged more than four hundred days in the last four years fishing for this trout—we love it.

A little over a hundred years ago, a fishing fool named J. F. Ellis assumed the job of U.S. Fisheries Commissioner. Mr. Ellis, lover of fight-ing fish, went on a European fishing tour at the government's expense. Besides slinging flies and lures in likely locations, he hit the 1880 International Fisheries Exposition in Berlin.

At the Expo, he met a soul mate named Baron Von Behr, president of the Deutsche Fishery Society. The good baron insisted that Commissioner Ellis visit the Black Forest and cast a line for his first real trout. The trip must have

Whirling Disease: The Least You Should Know

We all need to do our part to help prevent whirling disease, caused by a spore that attacks the cartilage and central nervous system of small fish. According to the Whirling Disease Foundation, it represents the single greatest threat to our native fish populations. If you are in whirling disease waters, you'll want to take special precautions to prevent it from spreading.

You are at greatest risk of transporting spores if you have been wading in a water known to carry this disease. It's easy to pick up the spores, which collect most heavily on the bottom, often in the sediment. Rinsing off your waders and boots is a first step, but it isn't enough—especially if they are felt-bottomed. Soak your boots and waders in the tub in 130-degree water for about fifteen minutes or in a bleach solution (1 to 10 ratio of bleach to water) for about ten minutes.

Whirling disease spores are tough little suckers that need to be respected. They can live for more than two months in a freezer. This is why rinsing and letting your boots air dry isn't enough. They will even survive being blasted in a microwave oven for over five minutes (not that we recommend doing this to your boots anyway). You can now buy wading boots with a treated sole that won't be as likely to trap spores.

For more information visit the Whirling Disease Foundation online at www.whirling-disease.org.

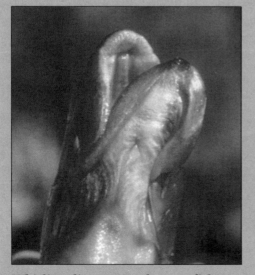

Whirling disease can damage fish cartilage and cause severe deformities.
—Beth MacConnell photo

Young rainbow trout show "black tail" symptoms from whirling disease. —R. Baury Nehring photo

Brown trout, once foreign to our waters, are here to stay.

been more than eventful. Ellis fell in love with this German game fish—a love affair he never outgrew.

He called the fish brown trout, cleverly naming them after their soft brown color. He felt a fish this good had to be imported stateside. Americans needed to have the best of everything after all—and that included the brown trout. In 1884 the Baron sent eighty thousand brown trout eggs on the Teutonic steamship *Werra*. The first browns were released on the north branch of the Pere Marquette River outside of Baldwin, Michigan, soon after their arrival.

About a year later another batch of fries were brought over from Scotland. These Scottish fish were called the Loch Leven browns, a still-water strain known to be excellent fighters.

Thus the German and the Loch Leven browns found new homes taking America by stream. After a while, the two fish interbred and the angler became the winner. Meanwhile, the brown established a firm foothold in New Zealand and South America, both places producing monster fish. Chile is one of the brown trout hot spots in the world today.

A brown trout is a thing of beauty. Depending on the water and the time of year, a fish

may have a deep chocolate hue or a light and more silvery hue; sometimes it's olive green or greenish bronze. Spots, accented by a light blue outer ring, adorn its head, back, and sides. Some of the spots on the sides show up a gorgeous deep red or light scarlet. The tail can have an orange tinge, and the belly has a yellow or creamy cast, the intensity and color depending on the water.

Younger fish have a somewhat forked tail; however, as the fish grows older it starts to square up. Old lunkers are often called squaretails by anxious anglers.

If humans were much smaller and browns much bigger, we'd not take swimming outdoors so lightly. Anglers have taken browns in low forty-pound range—which is one big fish! A record fish weighing 42.2 pounds was taken in 1970 in Arkansas. Several fish from Scotland have topped the scales at nearly 40 pounds. As a general rule, a brown will be about 4.5 times as long as it is deep. It's a water bullet, able to shoot out of cover at the speed of light to nab its prey.

Some of the largest browns in the United States have been taken out of the White River in Arkansas and Flaming Gorge Reservoir in Utah and Wyoming. Browns have done very well in tailwaters and as transplants. Because

Where we live, brown trout are our bread-and-butter fish. Within a few minutes of our homes, we can both be fishing blue-ribbon browns on the Provo River.

of the brown's versatility, it inhabits many waters and is an angler's favorite prey.

Browns are versatile fish, able to tolerate a wide variation in water temperature and seeming to thrive where other fish flounder. Ideally a brown likes water that is 54 to 64 degrees, although it can tolerate water in the low 40s to the high 70s better than most trout.

Spawn

Browns spawn in the fall—Michael and Alan's favorite time of the year. Depending on where you fish, the end of September to late November will bring on the best brown trout fishing of the year. Where we live in Utah, the spawn gets under way about the end of October and tapers off in December.

At this time, the normally careful brown trout goes mad and will hit about anything you throw. Since most fish are setting on redds (a fancy name for spawning beds) in one to three feet of water, use a small lure with just enough weight to get near the bottom but not enough to hang up. It helps to wear polarized glasses so you can see where the fish are. If you are standing below the redd, cast five to ten feet above the redd to get a good drift. Work the lure just faster than the current—just off the bottom. Fish it past the redd since other fish will wait below the redd for eggs that the current carries away.

If you are facing the redd in the current, cast across and over and work the lure toward you. Try to work each stretch of water carefully, and be aware that they go hot and cold. If you know you are on an active redd, keep fishing. If you aren't picking up any fish within fifteen or twenty minutes, try a different-colored lure. If that doesn't produce fish, move on, but try the redd again later.

Don't kill what you love. Be careful where you walk during the spawn. Avoid walking on redds—the gravelly areas. A careless foot could crunch thousands of brown trout eggs, your future fishing supply. Remember, too, that spawning fish are more prone to stress. Retrieve your fish as quickly as you can and release it. Don't keep spawning fish—let them go out and make baby fish!

Feeding Habits

While you might find browns anywhere in a stream if they are feeding, they prefer quiet pools and runs of clear water. Browns often hold close to the bank; we've seen plenty of big browns feeding just a few inches from shore.

Browns are cautious feeders for the most part and deserve the reputation they've earned of being the hardest trout in the water to hook. Browns, however, are less cautious after dark. They have a tendency to look something over before they take it. It's not unusual to have a brown take gentle nips at your lure—nips that send your blood racing but are impossible to hook up on.

Until they get larger and eat anything that crawls, swims, or flies, brown trout are primarily aquatic and terrestrial insect feeders. This makes them very accessible to the fly-fisher, but not out of reach for the spin caster. While an aggressive fish will take anything you throw in front of it, brown trout lures tend to have a slower action and be smaller than what one would use for other trout. Some of our favorites are Rooster Tails, Super Duper #503s, and a variety of small Mepps and Blue Fox spinners.

CUTTHROAT TROUT (*ONCORHYNCHUS CLARKI*)

This fish is named "cut" throat for the wonderful orange slash under its jaw. When you hook into this cold-water bulldog, it usually won't jump. It will dive for the deep water, pulling for all its worth.

Cutts can be the easiest fish in the world to catch—or they can shut down completely. When this fish gets selective in its feeding, catching it can be a real challenge. Nevertheless, the cutt is prone to overfishing and holds only in the purest waters. It was nearly wiped out at the turn of the twentieth century. There are a number of different strains, but pure strains, sadly, are few and far between nowadays. There are about fourteen subspecies, the Yellowstone, the Bear River, and the Snake River being some of the more recognizable.

The beautiful orange slash on the fish's jaw can be more or less pronounced depending on the strain, the water conditions, the time of year, or whether the fish has crossbred with its close cousin, the rainbow. The top of the trout is often a ripening-banana green.

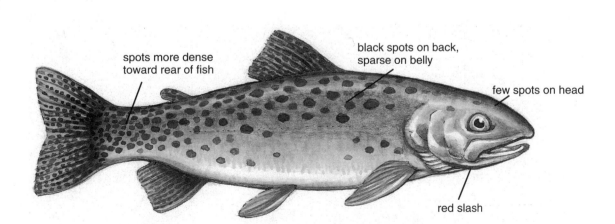

spots more dense toward rear of fish

black spots on back, sparse on belly

few spots on head

red slash

CUTTHROAT TROUT

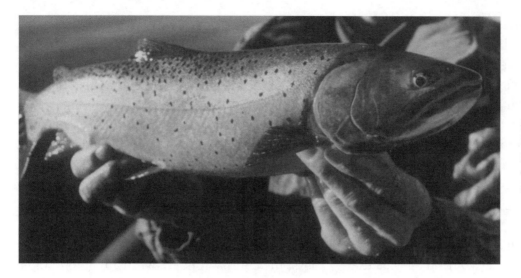

Cutthroat get their name from the bright orange slash below their jaw.

The biggest cutts may have gone the way of the buffalo. After the turn of the twentieth century in the Truckee/Tahoe area of the eastern Sierra Nevada, some very large fish were harvested commercially. It wasn't long until this fish was just a memory. The record fish, taken in Pyramid Lake, Nevada, weighed more than forty-one pounds. Most cutts today are under ten pounds. The body on the cutt is about five times as long as it is deep. The tail is slightly forked.

Cutthroats are sensitive and have more specific needs than browns or 'bows. Cutts want clean, fresh water. And like the grayling, the cutt is an environmental barometer—they like it pure. Cutthroats can survive in temperatures from 32 to 70 degrees–but they thrive in water between 52 to 59 degrees (give or take a few points). This is where they feel the most comfortable and where they feed the most actively—and where you'll catch the most fish.

Spawn

Cutts are easy and fun to catch during the spawn, but they are also more delicate then. You need to be careful with the resource. Bring them in quickly and release them gently. Take care not to walk on the spawning areas, or redds.

Cutts spawn in the spring. The spawn comes at different times in the spring depending on the water temperature, and it lasts off and on for about a month. When the stream waters reach about 50 degrees and the ice comes off the lakes, cutthroat trout start thinking family thoughts. Male and female cutts seek the riffles in shallower water with rocky bottoms. Lake fish will migrate up streams. The female fans out a nest and lays her eggs, which the male fertilizes. A female cutt will lay about one thousand eggs per pound.

During the spawn, bounce a Glo Bug through spawning grounds with enough shot to keep it deep. A red or white spinner will also produce good results. A Mepps or a white or black Panther Martin are especially good. Stand below the redd and cast above it, reeling just faster than the current.

Feeding Habits

Cutts as a rule aren't picky eaters. Cutthroat feed heavily on crustaceans and aquatic insects when they are young. As they grow older, they start terrorizing the fry population, feeding more on small fish. As cutts grow large, they feed on fish almost exclusively.

Cutthroats generally don't lie in the slow water that browns seem so fond of. Nor do they hang in the faster part of the stream where 'bows take refuge. To quote a friend, "they like the in-between zones." The cutthroat is closely related to the rainbow, and they share much of the same territory. Cutts, however, aren't as likely to be found lying in front of a rock or in the heaviest part of the riffle. Look for these fine fish in rocky areas, near rocks that break up the current, or on the downstream side of logjams. You can fish for cutts most anywhere in a small stream.

In lakes or ponds, look for cutts near structure. Moss lines are good fishing waters. Pay close attention to drop-offs, where these fish will hold. You'll also be successful if you work the points, peninsulas, and feeder streams. Structure is the key. Cutts will work the shorelines searching for food. If you can find where fish are feeding, cast to that section of water.

An aggressive cutthroat will take dang near anything. For this reason, some anglers consider cutts an easy fish to catch. And at times they can be. They will line up to get at your lure, and you can catch dozens and dozens of fish. Other times, though, this wonderful fish can be downright frustrating. The cutt, perhaps more than any other trout, can become selective. If the cutt fishing shuts down, selectivity

is usually the problem. If you can match your lure or fly to what the fish are eating, you will catch fish. If you can't, experiment with other strategies that might help. Try increasing or decreasing your retrieval of the lure. Also experiment with raising or lowering the lure position in the water. If this doesn't work, try several completely differently lures in a short period of time. Change strategies if the one you are using doesn't bring results. If you see a working fish continually feeding on the surface, keep casting to it. It might take your lure out of anger.

Almost any fly, lure, or jig can be effective on a cutt. As a rule, this fish tends to like flashy colors, especially red and white. Michael, our resident cutt expert, uses several lures almost exclusively for cutthroat fishing. His favorites, in order, are 1) Jake's Spin-a-Lure (silver or bronze, depending on the day), the best cutt lure ever made; 2) White Rooster Tail in various sizes, depending on the water and the size of the fish (other colors, especially black, work, but white is the best); 3) Super Duper #503; and 4) Mepps.

In cold water, fish the lure slowly—as slowly as you dare. Otherwise, you'll need to experiment with the lure speed. In streams, we

Cutthroat live in the cold, pure waters of the Rockies and the West Coast.

like to work upstream, casting up and pulling the lure a little faster than the current. Rooster Tails work great in small streams because they are light and don't sink too fast.

RAINBOW TROUT (*ONCHORHYNCHUS MYKISS*)

The rainbow is highly sought after and likely the first trout most of us caught in our childhood. This fish has enchanted the hearts of those who chase it. It's hard not to fall in love with the swirl of rainbow colors, the leaping hunk of channeled dynamite. No sooner do you set the hook then this fish goes airborne—partly in an effort to shake the hook, perhaps partly to impress you with its color and acrobatic skills. If you get sidetracked by the show and drop the rod tip or let slack creep into your line, the 'bow will shake your hook and leave you wondering why. The show was worth the battle, but you'll still be wanting.

As the name implies, this trout sports a gorgeous band of rainbow color on each side that becomes brighter and more distinct closer to spawning. Clear, cool, pure water also helps produce a brilliant color in this lovely fish.

The 'bow's back can have rather a green tint or it can be silverish. The belly is white. Black spots speckle the body and are more pronounced in cool water and during the spawn. It's enough to make you fall in love again.

Don't let the beauty of this fish fool you. It's also one of the biggest, line-pullingest fish in the aquatic underworld. Most of us feel pretty lucky if we get a 'bow over five pounds. However that's a drop in the bucket when you realize a 'bow can get into the fifty-pound range.

Perhaps not quite as hardy as the brown, the rainbow is still a very "durable" fish that lives in a wide variety of water types and temperatures. As a rule, it won't tolerate water quite as warm as the brown, but it can survive (barely) water temperatures in the very low 80s and as low as 31 degrees. Its preferred temperature range is between 55 and 65 degrees, with 58 to 60 degrees being the ideal temperature range.

Rainbows thrive on clean water and sections of the river that tend to be a little more oxygenated and a little faster than ideal brown trout habitat. While you often find browns in slower water, riffles and moving water are a good place to cast for 'bows.

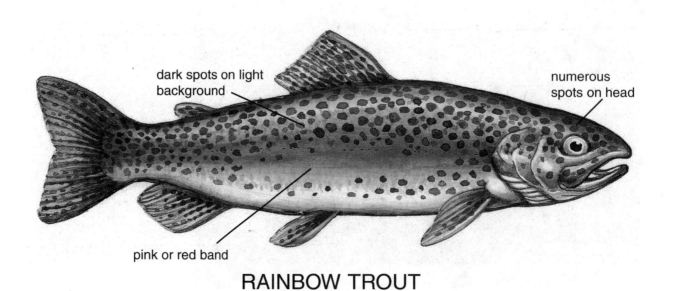

dark spots on light background

numerous spots on head

pink or red band

RAINBOW TROUT

Rainbow trout

Spawn

Rainbow spawn in the spring, and it is at this time of year you can hook a good one. However, depending on your location, the spring spawn can start as early as February or March or come as late as June. It all depends on the water conditions.

During the spawn, a Glo Bug, which is a piece of yarn on a fly, works about as well as anything. It isn't a spinner, but our job is to get you into fish. Tie on a Glo Bug and use enough weight to get it to the bottom and let it drift with the current. It's a great 'bow taker.

Feeding Habits

Rainbows weighing less than a pound feed almost exclusively on aquatic insects and crustaceans. Rainbows more than any other trout also feed on plants, both algal and vascular growths. As the 'bows grow, they become quite predatory, feeding more on other fish. Rainbows inhabit so many types of water it's hard to predict exactly what they will eat. They're very adaptable and seem to be less temperamental than their fellow trout. Some anglers say that 'bows will eat anything, but while rainbows have large appetites, you can be sure they also have discriminating taste.

Rainbows are very aggressive fish and, by trout standards, not easily spooked—you can get fairly close. When you hook into a 'bow, you have a real line puller. A rainbow is a shaker and a leaper. You have to keep your line taut. Planted hatchery fish are generally a stupid population and easy (too easy) to catch. Native rainbows present a fun challenge.

Rainbows like bright, gaudy colors, especially reds, and are attracted to flash. On streams, a Super Duper #503 in bronze or silver will work well. Panther Martins, Vibrax, and Blue Fox spinners are also good choices. Those lures will also work on lakes and ponds. However, if you are fishing big water, especially if you are trolling, add a few Flat Fish to your collection—they are wonderful rainbow attractors. If you are trying to catch large fish, consider trolling with lures that look like fish. Big 'bows find fish lures irresistible.

BROOK TROUT (*SALVELINUS FONTINALIS*)

The speckled trout, as the brookie is often called, has a lust for life. The brook trout is one of the loveliest fish God ever made. Of course, the brookie isn't really a trout at all but a char.

The brookie is native to eastern North America; however, it adapts to other regions handily as long as the water is cool and clean. The fish has always been a popular sport fish, so much so that many waters in New York and New England were all but fished out by the 1860s (soldiers had to have something to do in their off times).

Since brookies were almost fished to extinction, some farsighted anglers decided to do something. Seth Green, an early conservationist to whom we owe a great debt, started a hatchery. Seth was motivated by more than just conservation—he loved to catch brookies and started to release hatchery fish to supplement dwindling wild populations.

Nowadays, the brook trout is rooted firmly throughout the East and Canada, as well as the Rocky Mountains and West Coast drainages. You'll find it from Georgia to the Arctic. This fish is rather delicate compared to the rainbow, and its habitat requirements are more demanding than the 'bow and brown. Brookies can't tolerate temperature extremes or polluted water.

The brookie is a fighting fish with all the tenacity of a crew-cut marine sergeant. These fish are excellent sport and a truly great fishing experience.

A brook trout's colors are enough to make you believe it'll be in heaven. The bottom of the fins are reddish golden, outlined in black and white. The back of the brookie is a rather interesting dark green to cocoa black with little wavy lines (like wood eaten by a worm) called vermiculation. This color flattens out on the sides, which host various shades of reddish spots rimmed in blue, sometimes interspersed with yellow spots. When the males spawn, their belly turns a delicate orange.

If you latch into a four- or five-pound brook trout, consider yourself pretty dang lucky. Nowadays a fish in the two- to three-pound class is a fine fish—the average fish being

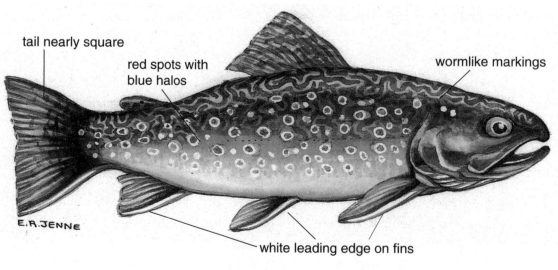

tail nearly square

red spots with blue halos

wormlike markings

white leading edge on fins

E.R.JENNE

BROOK TROUT

Big brookies like this haunt many Canadian waters. —Daniel Collins photo

around one pound. For truly large brookies, an angler needs to head to Canada and fish Manitoba, Ontario, or Labrador. Such virgin waters haven't been fished out and a larger strain of fish still haunts the waters. In pure Canadian waters, a good angler can latch into fish five to eight pounds, and up to ten pounds is not impossible. The Nipigon River in Ontario is one of the best places to fish for large brook trout. Wyoming is a great place in the West to try for really good brookies. Most of the brookies in non-native waters tend to be rather small as a result of genetic inferiority.

As a general rule, a brook trout will be about five times as long as it is deep.

Big fish need a lot of water to thrive. The largest fish will be in larger streams and open waters. Brook trout prefer water temperatures around 58 degrees, but can tolerate water as cold as 43 degrees or as warm as 72 degrees. While this fish is fairly delicate, it can take water with a higher alkalinity and acid content than either 'bows or cutts.

Spawn

The spawn occurs from September to December depending on the location of the water and the temperature. Brook trout won't attack a Glo Bug as readily as a rainbow will, but it's still a good choice for brookies. A white or black Rooster Tail or a small, chartreuse Mister Twister are good lure choices for catching brook trout during the spawn.

Feeding Habits

Some anglers have suggested that brookies are easy to catch, almost stupid. When we've been in Yellowstone National Park or the High Uinta Mountains of Utah, especially in the backcountry, we hear a lot of anglers talking about how easy it is to hook into these little powerhouses. At times it might seem that this fish is easy to catch, but that's not really accurate. When the brookie population gets a little overpopulated, fish get very hungry and not very selective. Many fish in mountain waters are half starved and will take anything. It makes for good fishing. Also, in waters like this, you're doing the population a favor by taking out a limit to eat.

If the fish seem selective, vary the retrieve on your lure, retrieving faster or slower. Or stop action completely, then retrieve, stop the action, then retrieve, and so on. Our all-time favorite lures for fishing brook trout are the Super Duper #503 silver, the Jake's Spin-a-Lure, and a selection of Mepps.

The beautifully colored brook trout are tiny bundles of fishing joy.

13
COVER YOUR BASS
Tips on Taking Ol' Bucketmouth and Smallmouth

We were once trout-fishing snobs, but that's in the past. If it has fins and will take a lure, we'll go for it (okay, maybe not carp). Like a lot of trout boys, we were too limited in days of yore. The casting sun rises and set on lots of different fish.

Changes are good. The nice thing is that at different times of year you can fish for different species. This gives you a chance to change the playing field and go for different fish.

We were introduced to the excitement of bass fishing a number of years ago. Michael caught his first bass twenty-five years ago in east Texas. Alan hooked his first more than a decade ago.

You could say we've made up for lost time since our late arrival into the fold of the bass faithful. We fish a lot of bass these days, often when the trout water looks less than promising. The highlight of the year, however, is our

Michael mysteriously catches more bass than Alan, but Alan always lands the lunkers.

annual "Cover Your Bass" competition, where we determine who is the best bass boy and who has the bragging rights until the next contest. It's bloody, it's dirty, it's serious business. It's also great fun.

Let's take a look at Mr. Bass, a favorite sport fish and growing more popular each year. You might think that since professional bass anglers make such big bucks, bass fishing is a tough operation—limited to the few. Well, there's nothing mystical about being a successful bass angler.

With game fish like bass, you have to labor under the assumption that big fish munch on little fish. There's no such thing as species loyalty. About the only rule a bass labors under is it has to be able to get the food in its mouth. Whether it can actually swallow its prey or not is something it'll worry about later.

To say that bass are predatory is to damn with faint praise. Bass are vicious, opportunistic creatures with little more on their minds than where the next meal is coming from.

LARGEMOUTH BASS

Bass have really big mouths. In fact the choppers extend beyond a bass's beady eyes. We've both hooked tiny little bass that were trying to swallow lures bigger than their own body size. If a largemouth (also called bucketmouth) bass were the size of a small shark, it would take on a Jet Ski, no doubt thinking it was a new style of buzzbait.

Once at a small lake in east Texas (remaining nameless on purpose), we had a most unusual experience fishing for largemouth bass. Dodging the water moccasins, which were as thick as mosquitoes, we launched our boat and began working some weeds. After a few casts, a small water moccasin swam across the water about ten yards in front of us. Out of nowhere, a bass the size of a small jake turkey shot out of the water and gulped that viper down. We'd

The bucketmouth has got to be one of the few fish in the world with a maw big enough to swallow itself.

heard a bass would munch a snake, but this was the first time we'd ever seen it. We weren't sad to see one less moccasin, but now other, more painful visions of death crept into our minds.

As most outdoor sorts are prone to do, we watched the beauties of God's nature while we fished. In particular, there was a plump mallard hen with a clutch of five half-grown chicks that kept swimming past us from one set of reeds to the next. After a while, we noticed there were only four chicks. We figured the odd one was lost (ducks aren't Rhodes Scholars, you know). Around 3:00 P.M. we stopped to take in some life-sustaining liquid, Classic Coke, since the day was hot. After a third can each, the same fat duck with her family came scooting across the water in front of us, apparently unconcerned about her lost baby.

In what first came as a ripple and then a minor tidal wave, a gray-green-brown mass erupted through the water and gulped home a half-grown duck. The bucketmouth did it as easily as we had finished the last gulp of Coke just a minute earlier.

HILDA, THE AMAZING FISHING CHICKEN OF PICKAWAY COUNTY, OHIO

We were amazed. Not only because the fish was the size of Cleveland but also by the raw power and pluck of such a creature. We swore many oaths to catch it. We caught many bass that day. We were also a little paranoid, looking in the mouth of each to make sure there wasn't a water moccasin poised to strike when we fetched out the hook.

Going to the Food

There are two reasons why shallow water provides good bass fishing. One, the water temperature is comfortable. Two, shallower water is the best dining room—where the dinner bell tolls. Largemouth bass love to eat. The largemouth is an ambusher—built for dash, not distance. When a bass strikes, there's nothing half-hearted about it. When bass fishing is hot, it's the best kind of adrenaline rush.

A bass hides in a likely spot, waits, and ambushes food as it comes by. The key is knowing how the bucketmouth bass itself fishes. Wait. Ambush. Wait. Ambush. Look for structure where a bass might hold for protection or hide. When you fish, you need to look at the water as if you were a lunker bass with a big mouth and stomach to match.

Like trout and other game fish, bass travel in feeding lanes—established travel paths between feeding and holding areas (from deeper to shallower water, from bedroom to kitchen). Look for where a largemouth bass might hold when it's not feeding, where it might feed, and some of the likely travel routes Mr. and Mrs. Bass might haunt. Then fish those feeding lanes.

One of the main reasons why Alan is a good bass fisherman (tourneys be damned) is he

Bass don't nibble anything—they ambush like a guerrilla soldier and hit like a freight train.

really knows how to read bass water. He thinks like a bass and understands where bass feed and where they hold. He's also good at judging the lanes and fishing them.

How to Catch Largemouth Bass Consistently

We've discussed following the food—a key element in having a close encounter of the bass kind. We've also suggested that it's critical that you understand the nature of a bass.

Fish around, over, and through the Structure

Unless you catch a bucketmouth bass in a feeding lane, you'll be wasting your time if you don't fish the structure where a bass holds, waiting to ambush its dinner.

Arguably the Best *Really Big* Bass Lakes in the Lower Forty-Eight

When it gets down to bass, there are fist fights over what water is the best. According to our research and personal experience, here are some of the best lakes in which to catch really big bass.

- **Lake Minnetonka, Minnesota. 13,999 lovely acres of water, a lot of structure, and excellent fishing.**

- **Castaic Lake, California. 2,500 acres; 17-pounders are more than possible.**

- **Lake Okeechobee, Florida. 700 square miles; 40-bass days are not at all uncommon, nor are 6-pound fish. Better have a boat.**

- **Lake Fork, Texas. 22,690 acres; a lot of 10-pound fish and home of many records, including the 17-plus-pound fish at Pro Bass.**

- **Lake Pleasant, Arizona. 10,500 acres, lots of 10-pounders, and hot action.**

- **Lake Seminole, Georgia. 38,000 acres of bass heaven. A hot lake with charm.**

Alan likes to look at maps of the lake bottom before he fishes a water. This gives him an initial idea of the structure of the lake—where old creek bottoms are, where the lake drops, where there might be rocky structures. He's also been known to strap on his dive mask and plunk his face under the surface.

A map isn't always possible or practical. Look for other structures where a bass might hide, such as fallen logs or trees, beaver dams, a rock slide, a weed line, lily pads, the shade of a tree or brush, and undercut banks. A bass likes to feel it can't be seen from above. Also look for any shade beneath or on top of the water.

Shorebirds eating bugs or minnows are good indicators of where largemouth bass might be. In the early morning or late evening, try topwater lures near likely places. For that matter, try them as the day warms, too, although they often won't produce as well.

If a bass is working the surface, pay close attention to where the action is. Look for big splashes; the bass won't be far away. Active fish are exciting and usually relatively easy to catch. At least the two big problems are covered—you know about where the fish is and that the fish is hungry.

When you find an active fish or some promising structure, determine where you think the optimum strike zone is. If you see a fish actively working the area, cast over the strike zone and work your lure across it politely. If the fish likes what you are offering for lunch, it'll respond. Repeat the process several times and then work both sides of the zone until you're sure you've covered the area. If this hasn't produced a fish, try a different lure.

If you're fishing what looks to be a likely piece of water, mentally mark the strike zones. Start at the edge and overcast so your lure is actively working when it comes into the area in question. Work the area from side to side. If this hasn't produced a fish, tie on another lure if you have a good feeling about the place, or move to the next area.

This water is prime bass habitat.

There's a lot of water to cover. Don't fall into the trap of working the same water too long. You are better off with a shotgun approach, trying a number of different spots.

Put life in your lure by varying the retrieve. Experiment with how you drag the hardware. Start off by working it slow and erratic. If you are trying to simulate a wounded or dying fish, how would it look in the water? It likely wouldn't be swimming in a straight line at the same speed. There would be some starts and stops. It's a consummate act of bravery for a tiny fish to swim in open water with a monster bass or other game fish ready to eat it. A small fish is spooky.

Now let's go into more detail. To really understand the largemouth bass, you have to understand a little more about its specific needs and how these change from season to season, for example, where and when you fish spring bass and how different it will be from summer or winter bass.

Fishing for Largemouth Bass in Fall and Spring (Cooling to Semiwarm Water)

When you get to the fringes of either season, things overlap, so the following discussion will be general; however, you'll get the idea. There are a lot of variables, but the principles hold true.

The key to success in fall and spring is fishing shoreline water. After winter the cold water starts to warm up. After summer, with winter coming on, the water starts to cool down. Thus, the shallower water near the shoreline maintains a more comfortable temperature for a bucketmouth bass. It's the last water to feel winter's bite and it's the first water to warm after ice-off (if you're fishing an area of cold winters).

As you know, the shoreline, besides being more comfortable for largemouth bass is a moveable feast of insects and fish fry. In this water, a bass feels comfortable and will get an appetite back after a long winter. In the spring, a bass will go on a feeding binge to put on all the extra ounces it can. In fall, it will eat anything that's not nailed down, preparing for the somewhat dormant winter months. It's nature's way of saving on the food bill.

When fishing shallow water with a lot of structure, work the water carefully so you don't overlook any hiding places. If the water is still a little chilly, fish lures that you can pull through

Bass feed near shore. This shoreline and the line of grass in the middle of the water will be good bass fishing.

the water slowly. If you rip the lure too fast, Mr. Bass won't have the energy to play games with you.

In early spring or late fall, you may also need to shift to a smaller piece of hardware. You'll have to experiment to see what works best in your favorite waters.

If traditional hardware isn't working, take a few tips from fly rodders and tie on a fly. Use an egg sinker, a swivel, and leader. Try a bulky leech pattern, a frog pattern, or a Muddler minnow. A Muddler is a great item to have in your tackle since it represents so many things. You can use it as a leech, as a sculpin (which is what it was designed to imitate), as a general minnow pattern, or on the surface as a hopper. Michael confesses now, for the first time, that during every "Cover Your Bass" contest in which he's taken Alan to the cleaners, he's used a Muddler at least half the time. The Muddler is out of the bag.

While bigger bass flies were theoretically designed for fly rods, you can fish them very effectively with a spinning rod. Keep in mind, you give the fly its action.

Every tackle box should have a selection of $\frac{1}{16}$-, $\frac{1}{4}$-, and $\frac{1}{2}$-ounce marabou and bucktail jigs in a variety of colors. Have a selection of weedless hooks on hand, too. This is one of the best all-around game fish–getting lures. Like the Muddler, jigs imitate any number of things, from leeches to minnows to nymphs. Don't leave home without them. Michael tends to favor black and olive with bulky bodies and long tails. Alan has better luck with flashy colors and more sparsely tied bodies.

Don't even think of heading out on a bass trip without taking along a few different sizes of crayfish imitations. These little creatures are the bass version of a McDonald's Happy Meal. Work them as slow as you think you can, and then slow it down some more—you'll be about right. Crayfish don't move nearly as fast as casters seem to think they do, and bass pay no attention whatsoever to those that swim like they're attached to rocket boosters.

Fishing for Largemouth Bass in Winter (Cold Water)

When the water starts to get colder, you have to remember one simple thing. The fish really slow down. If you want to break those chilly winter bass blues and latch into a few pounds of fighting fins, so must your methods slow down.

As with most game fish, bucketmouth bass in the winter are a cross between an NFL couch potato and a hibernating grizzly bear. Thus, a fast retrieve may not excite a largemouth because it's too much work to pursue. The method that worked a bass to frenetic frenzy last summer will likely be a big turnoff now. When in doubt, slow it down. You need to make your lure presence known in a positive, yet subtle, sort of way. Be patient and be prepared to drag your lure past Mrs. Bass's nose, so all she has to do is open that magnificent maw.

Fishing for Largemouth Bass in Summer (Warm Water)

When the shoreline water reaches the low to mid 70s, bass magic begins. In our part of the world, this happens in the summer; in warmer climates, it's earlier. As long as the water temperature stays in this range, the fishing will be good.

As the water temperature starts to climb beyond this, exciting bass action begins to taper off accordingly. In the spring and fall, it's a good strategy to sleep in, then hit the water after a good breakfast. In the summer, you'll need to adjust your timing. As the water warms and the temperatures climb, early mornings and late evenings (and through the night where it's legal) provide the best largemouth bass fishing.

The shoreline water won't be as comfortable, so the bass will go there to eat, then scoot back to the comforts of cooler, deeper water. While they won't be staying in the shallow water any longer than they have to, they're hungry and aggressive. Every now and then the fishing action gets hot. But as a rule, it's slower fishing.

In the summer it's necessary to fish the structure heavily and look for working fish. A working fish will be your highest percentage hook-up.

On a hot day when the fish are dug in deep, a slow spinner may be just the thing to coax an attack.

Fishing for Largemouth Bass during the Spawn

If you want to feel like a bass pro, fish the spawn. All the cunning and wariness that nature has provided bass with goes out the back window when love is in the water. At this time, a bass is so cocky it would take on a mako shark. It ain't afraid of nothin', especially a crankbait worked in front of it.

Pre-spawn fishing is fun and exciting. When the temperature hits the middle to high 50s, largemouth bass start to drift toward the shoreline and bask in the shallower water. It's time to put on the feed bag to fuel up for the courting. The sloppier your cast and the more splash you make, the madder they get and the harder they fight.

You need to hit it hard during the pre-spawn period to make up for those bass dry spells that come later on during the year. At this time of the year, we recommend you catch and release your bass unless you hook one so badly it will die. Get them back out there making more bass babies. Put off the die and fry—at least for now. Protect your resources.

Bucketmouths will begin to spawn when the water temperature reaches the low to mid 60s. During the spawn, bass daddies go out of their way to achieve domestic equality. They build the home—a nest in sand, gravel, vegetation, or mats of grass—and guard it viciously. The dad makes a half-circle depression about two to four feet wide and five to ten inches deep.

Mrs. Bass lays her 25,000 to 45,000 eggs (big families, these bass). After this, she takes off and has a deep-water holiday—leaving the kiddies to daddy. In a week or two, depending on how cold the water is, baby bass start to hatch. The male fans the nest with his tail to oxygenate the eggs. During this time, the male takes on anything smaller than a submarine that comes near his nest. If it's your lure, you have a fight on your hands. It does have to get near his nest, however. He's not going to go very far out of his way to get it because he can't leave the eggs. After the babies hatch, he, too, takes off to the deep water for a vacation.

After the spawn, bass go on another feeding frenzy to replenish the calories they lost during the baby-making process. This is an excellent time to fish. In our experience, a post-spawn bass will take on any lure. Size, shape, action, and color don't seem to matter; if it moves, it's lunch.

Smallmouth Bass

Don't let the word *smallmouth* throw you. It's called a smallmouth, but its mouth is pretty large. More than once we've landed fish that had crayfish or fish nearly as big as themselves stuffed in their gullet. Even a small smallmouth can gobble a pretty big lure. And a smallmouth bass is one of the fightingest fish you're liable to hook up with. But be forewarned: fishing for this little critter is addictive.

Smallmouth, by the way, are also great table fare—if the population is thriving, we always keep a few for a good fry. It usually doesn't hurt to take a few home every now and again.

Smallmouth don't seem to nibble. They attack their food like hungry saber-toothed cats. This fish doesn't get the press the largemouth does, nor is it quite as widespread, since it has specific water demands. At one time, the smallmouth called the Ohio River and Lake Ontario systems home. But you can't keep a good thing, or a good fish, on the farm. To date, you can find smallmouth in varying degrees in every state except Hawaii, Alaska, Florida, and Louisiana. The smallmouth has been a stocking success. In fact, rumor has it that buckets of smallmouth crossed the Alleghenies roped to the outside of a train, destined for future waters.

Most fish will be from the half-to two-pound range. A fish from two to four pounds isn't out of the ordinary in good water; a fish over five pounds is in the trophy class. The largest fish

A smallmouth bass

on record weighed in at just over twelve pounds.

You can distinguish a smallmouth from a largemouth quite easily. If the mouth extends beyond the fish's eye, it's a largemouth. You'll note that a smallmouth bass also has very large eyes and spots on the sides. It's greenish with a hint of copper. In clear waters like the Umpqua River in Oregon, the fish are very bright and colorful.

For the first two years of a smallmouth's life, it eats mainly aquatic insects. By the time it's in its third year, and about eight inches long, aquatic insects aren't as important a food source. Smallmouth now focus on small minnows and crustaceans. They will eat most any minnow they can get in their mouth; however, they are especially interested in minnows that seem wounded or don't swim quite right. Make your lure look like a wounded fish.

Crayfish are one of the smallmouth's favorite foods, especially during the peak of the summer. We've found a smallmouth will take a cray any way it can get it, but it seems to prefer smaller crayfish. Molting crays, defenseless while the new shell is forming, are the greatest prize. They also give off a handy scent, released like wafting dinner odors, so a fish just follows its nose. From July through September, crayfish make up about 70 to 80 percent of this fish's diet.

How to Fish Smallmouth Bass Consistently

If you want to fish for smallmouth, you have to fish around structures such as boulders, ledges, cliff, rock walls, and snags. As always, locate where the fish feel comfortable. The Umpqua River in Oregon, for example, flows over an old lava bed. It's all rock. There are boulders, shelves, and cliffs—perfect places for smallmouth. In the clear water you can see the bottom and watch the fish hold next to the structure within the shadows of the rock.

When we fished the Umpqua, we learned it was best to work our lures around the edges first and then work the bottom with crayfish patterns and minnowlike lures. Anything this fish can get in its mouth is fair game. Smallmouth school up so where you catch one, you'll typically catch several. In a ten-yard area, we caught more than twenty good fish.

On lakes, fish the rocky edges, especially if there are drop-offs. If you aren't catching fish, fish deeper but count the lure down so once you've located the right depth, you'll be able to get there on each cast.

Seasonal Considerations

This fish likes rocky, clear water from 61 to 78 degrees. It's a fairly hearty little critter. As a rule, it's not as selective as a trout, nor as moody if the temperature is right. When the water cools, however, smallmouth shut down, and you'll need all your skill just to get a nod. Frankly, at this time, we don't worry about fishing this underwater football.

When the water warms, smallmouth get very active and will eat about anything. There is no perfect lure. We've used about every lure you can think of, all with about equal success. For days they want a lot of flash, a spoon is great. Other days they want something subtle, and a Rooster Tail or a small Panther Martin work well. On other days, a grub or a plastic worm is also very good.

When the water gets between 59 and 61 degrees, smallmouth spawn in flat, rocky, or gravelly water from three to ten feet deep. The fish will retreat after spawning to water a little bit deeper—from eight to fourteen feet deep. At this time, they will seek shoals, drop-offs and ledges, boulders, and even weed beds.

During the summer, as long as the water stays in the high 60s to the low 70s, fish will hold in ten to thirty-five feet of water with plenty of structure, ledges, drop-offs, weed beds, or shoals. In the cooler spring or fall, when the surface temperature is in the low 50s or less, bass will start to hold on flatter bottoms in thirty-five feet or more of water.

Favorite Bass Lures

Here are a few suggestions for your tackle box. While we've suggested some lures for lakes, that doesn't mean they might not also be successful in rivers or streams. Experiment to see what works for you. For example, Alan swears by a crankbait; Michael rarely uses one and prefers to use a spinner or jig.

Perhaps the best all-around lure is the jig tipped with a twister tail, a tube tail, or a plastic worm. These work in any water at any time of the year. A jig with a soft tail suggests hellgrammites, a number of minnows, or darters. A tube jig is a great crayfish imitation. The soft, chewable tail resembles a natural food item and triggers fish to strike more violently. You can put different weighted heads on the jig for different water situations. The best single color is chartreuse, followed by salt and pepper, sunburst purple, or black.

When fishing for smallmouths in lakes, try fishing crankbaits, floating Rapalas, Thin-Minnow lures, Plastic Shads, or jigs such as twister tails and tube tails.

In rivers and streams, jig twister tails, Thin-Minnow lures, crayfish crankbaits, and crankbaits all work well.

14

THE INCREDIBLE NORTHERN PIKE
The Northern Water Wolf

Whatever you call a northern pike—a water wolf, a northern, a pike, a pickerel, a jack, a Canadian jack—say it with respect. Few finned foe are more fun to fish or stronger fighters in the water.

Nature designed pike for killing. When you think of pike, you think of teeth—lots and lots of teeth. A pike doesn't feed, it attacks. It'll eat anything as long as its prey is at least a half inch shorter than itself and can fit in that jagged jaw.

Pike might hunt alone or in a pack in a sort of delicate alliance, there being no loyalty to its own kind. Like Washington, D.C., reporters, pike will turn on pike or anything slightly helpless, without remorse. If you pull a pike out of a hole or pool where they've packed up, it's not unusual for it to be missing chunks of flesh. Other fish, sensing the caught pike's dis-

advantage, turn on their own. It is nearly impossible to find a fish over five pounds that isn't covered with scars from numerous fights or near-death experiences. In this fish's world, it's kill and avoid being eaten. You grow big by being very, very aggressive. They play a deadly game of king of the hill.

The first thing you have to remember about pike is they are either aggressive or neutral. When the water reaches the mid-40s in the spring, northern pike start thinking about the spawn. During this time, they also start to tie on the feed bag—eating everything in sight. When the warmer water stirs their blood and they become active, the fishing gets very good. You'll need a good rest the night before so you'll have the strength to land lots of fish. During the spring, which in a pike's world can be from

Pike teeth. It's a very good idea to use pliers when taking out the hook.

Look at the mouth on this water wolf.

late April to as late as mid-June in some northern parts, these toothed lovelies head for the warmer and more comfortable shallow water. Pike haunt swampy areas, sloughs, backwaters, inlets with small entrances, mouths of warm feeder streams, and shallow, weedy edges of lakes and rivers.

Since the water is shallow, pike can be aggressive and spooky at the same time (usually spookiness isn't an adjective one would use to describe pike). In this warmer water they feed on small fish that are also flourishing in the warm temperature, and they'll munch on any large fish that foolishly come their way. Hungry and opportunistic, they will eat frogs, snakes, baby ducks, and rodents—anything that gets near those big jaws.

Usually you'll find pike alone in the really shallow water. As the water gets deeper, they group up. It's always a good strategy to assume that if you catch one fish in a spot, there's another one lurking nearby. Continue casting. Unlike some fish species, where catching a fish frightens the others, it's a dinner bell for pike.

You have to experiment. The water can change from day to day. Pike love fallen logs, the shade of the weeds near the edge, lips or drop-offs, hanging branches, boulders, seams with a riffle, and even the shadow of a boat. These fish won't feel comfortable unless partly hidden.

Fish to the structure. Cast up on bank if you have to, and pull the lure into the water with a big splash. For pike, a big splash where your lure plunks in gets the same reaction as a food vendor at a ball game yelling "hot dogs!"

In the summer as the water warms up, pike move into deeper water where it's more comfortable. They will still come into the shallows to feed, but they won't stay there for long. At times like this, look for transitional waters between the deeper water and the shallows. They prefer staying in this water, if possible, shooting into the shallows only to make a kill.

HOW TO FISH FOR PIKE EFFECTIVELY

Pike Moods

When pike are aggressive they'll take about anything you throw at them. However, every now and then they head to deeper waters and just shut down. This can come on in an instant

Fish as close to the line of grass as possible for pike holding in the vegetation.

TURNING THE TABLES

and last for several days. One year we'd caught boatloads of spring fish. It was too easy. The next day, for some reason, everything just went flat. We fished for nearly eight hours with only a few pike and some walleye for our trouble.

This shook our confidence. We'd been spotting fish for days in a number of shallow holding areas. Nothing hit! This sort of thing usually only happened in the summer when the water warmed up. We needed a new game plan.

You can't let a fish get the better of you. We put our heads together and fought back. We abandoned the traditional shallow-water, edge-of-river areas and decided to fish deeper pools. Instead of big spoons, we switched to $\frac{1}{2}$- and $\frac{1}{3}$-ounce spoons and jig heads.

The trick was to drag the lure right in front of the pouting fish's nose very, very slowly. We would go to the fish with a full-court press. Where the current allowed, we vertical jigged our twister tails. Instead of a couple of fish in eight hours, we caught a fish or two an hour. The fishing wasn't fast, by spring Canadian pike standards in great water, but we were catching fish.

Spring and Fall

Pike fishing in the spring and fall is about the same. Other than the spawn, there's not a lot of difference.

In the shallows before and during the spring spawn, pike are starting to build strength. Cold water is warming but is not optimal yet. This fish will likely be a little lethargic and not yet aggressive. It's still hungry, you can be sure, but not ready to do a lot of chasing and calorie burning. At times like this, pike may or may not be spooky but will surely be a little lethargic. You'll want to fish accordingly. Go smaller and slower.

Twitch and work a smaller lure on the surface to prevent hangups and provide maximum visibility for the fish. Let the lure dance and hover to give the fish time to take it. Even during the best of times, pike miss a fair number of lures when they strike.

If the lure is moving slowly, a lethargic fish will come over to investigate. If it moves too fast, it will let it go. Of course, getting the lure to the fish's nose is the best scenario; however, unless you're casting to a fish you see, this isn't

Our good friend Chuck Graves, an outfitter out of Fort McMurray, Alberta, holds a fine pike.

miss a few fish because of the setup, but you'll catch more fish in the long run since you'll fish more and have a lot fewer snags and weed problems. Also, a weedless lure is easier to cast on the bank and plop into the water if a fish is holding right on the bank.

In the spring, also look for weedy banks, fallen logs, pool edges, shallow water near banks, or any other area in which a pike could feed.

Summer Waters

As the water warms and weeds grow up in the shallows and the spring water recedes, the pike move into deeper water. To seek comfortable temperatures, the fish they are feeding on have gone a little deeper, too. You can still catch

always possible. When the water warms up and fish are feeling feisty, a bigger lure is, of course, in order for fishing in the deeper water.

Look for spawning areas such as backwater inlets with a small entry. These waters warm up quickly and attract pike like a magnet. They are excellent fishing, but inlets sometimes produce spooky fish. One time in Alberta, we fished an inlet with our friend Chuck. We could barely get the boat through the mouth even though the water opened up nicely once we got inside. Surprisingly, the temperature was 10 to 15 degrees warmer than the river—and packed with pike.

In several hours, we caught and released over forty fish among the logjammed waters. It was pike heaven. For spooky pike, few things work better than a jig with a plastic tail or a big, feathery fly with a little weight so you can cast it with a spinning rod. Small spoons and floating fishlike lures that don't hang up are very effective. In areas thick with brush and logs, consider taking the treble hooks off your floating lures and replacing them with single hooks. And since you're fishing in a lot of structure, a weedless hook makes sense. Sure you'll

This feisty nineteen-pound Canadian pike, caught by ten-year-old Jon-Michael, was a great trophy—and his first.

fish in the shallow water in the morning and evening around structure, but they won't hold there.

Fish for feeding pike that wait in the transitional water between the shallow and deep zones and dart into the shallows for a kill. Also, fish weed lines, recessed weed patches, and drop-offs.

In this water, you may want to use a bigger, heavier lure. Countdown baits are very effective, and if you are fishing in or near the weeds, a weedless lure is still a must.

Lures to Consider

Don't overdo the shark tackle. Pike get large, but half the challenge is taking them on light tackle. You need a medium-action rod like the Sage 470 and a reel with a large line capacity in case you hook into a really big fish. Depending on the conditions, 10- to 20-pound-test line is more than adequate.

Things that look like fish will bring in the pike. Almost any lure will work on an aggressive fish. Here are some of our favorites.

Spoons. Spoons have traditionally caught more northern pike than any other lure. Favorite sizes are the $\frac{3}{4}$- to $1\frac{1}{4}$-ounce in red-white and yellow-red (five of diamonds). Dardevles are the old standbys, but Luhr Jensen, Johnson, and Blue Fox also make good ones.

You can fish a spoon a number of ways, from deep to shallow and from fast to slow. A spoon is also great for jigging or splashing across the surface like a buzzbait.

A brisk retrieve is best for aggressive fish. (By the way, if you see a fish chasing your lure, don't slow the retrieve.) In cooler water or for neutral fish, work the spoon more slowly. Use your rod tip to guide the lure around in the water (figure eights, for example) to try and tempt the fish. To really entice a neutral fish, add a bit of pork belly, pike belly, or other bait to the lure.

Jigs/Plastic-tail Jigs. Jigs simply suggest food to a fish and are especially effective on slow days. Rubber-tailed jigs drive pike wild. Have a supply of $\frac{1}{4}$- to 1-ounce jigs with rubber tails that vary in length, shape, and color (black,

This small northern took our fly with a vengeance.

white, chartreuse, and smoky). Marabou jigs are also very good. Cast and retrieve or vertical jig in deeper water.

Fishlike Lures. Anything that looks like a fish will provoke a strike. Depending on the conditions, you'll want some surface lures and some that count down. We don't have an absolute favorite, although we carry a supply of Bullets, Cicadas, Ripple Tails, and Rapalas. If you can get one of these to a neutral pike's nose, you'll have a fish on.

Spinnerbaits. It's nice to have a few of these about on hot spring days when the pike are going nuts. Go for a $\frac{1}{2}$- to 1-ounce size. In a pinch, you can dance a spoon across the water like a spinnerbait.

Flies. For pike, big bass flies with lots of body that undulate in the water are great. Try a big Muddler Minnow. You'll need to add a little weight to cast, but work these flies in the water like a dancing jig.

15
Chasing Salmon and Steelhead
A Legal Addiction

No drug is more addictive than salmon or steelhead fishing. Michael grew up in the middle of salmon and steelhead country in southern Oregon. He cut his teeth on the Rogue River, one of the best waters in the world. His mother still isn't sure how many days of school he missed because of salmon and steelhead. It was a lot.

Salmon Species

There are five wonderful species of salmon to catch out West. We love them all. We love being in their company. We love fighting them. We love landing them. We love marinating, grilling, and eating them.

At the top of the salmon family tree is the chinook or king salmon. Large spring chinook are also known as Tyee in Canada. These trophy fish are worth their weight in gold to the serious salmon angler, and because of their power and size they have earned a reputation as tackle busters. Any king over 50 pounds is considered a noteworthy catch. Alaskan kings have been known to tip the scale at over 80 pounds, and a commercial fishing outfit once pulled in a 126-pound king on its way to Rivers Inlet.

A native of the Pacific Northwest, Michael was weaned on steelhead and raised on salmon—and still loves to fish for both.

Coho, or silver, salmon look almost identical to chinook but are a bit smaller, maxing out at around twenty-five pounds. They start entering rivers in late August, and in many waters it's not unusual to fish chinook and coho simultaneously. Coho have historically been the choice of anglers because of their abundance, quality, and accessibility, but numbers have dwindled in recent years and serious conservation measures are under way. We say love 'em and leave 'em; max out your limits on other species.

Sockeye salmon, or reds, are the fish often portrayed in documentaries about spawning salmon. They are smaller, ranging from four to twelve pounds, but pound for pound they are definitely one of the best-fighting freshwater fish you can ever hook—comparable to summer steelhead. They spawn in the millions, so catch and release is the strategy to take for a long late-summer weekend. No sense limiting out in the first half hour.

Chum salmon is one of the largest and strongest salmon and puts up a worthy battle when hooked. They aren't known for going airborne when hooked, but when they get their nose down into the deep water the fight will tire you both out. Chum isn't a great eating fish, so release these beasts after a battle and a photo.

Pink salmon, or humpies, are the smallest salmon, on average ranging from three to five pounds. They are somewhat fatter than other species and have an exaggerated humped back, as the name suggests. These salmon spawn only on odd-numbered years (1999, 2001, etc.) and enter the rivers in September. Pinks are easy to catch using just about any technique. We've found that flashy silver spinners work well.

STEELHEAD

Cult steelheaders make the folks who follow the Grateful Dead, the so-called "deadheads," look like a bunch of cub scouts. We aren't deadheads, we're *steel*heads. A steelhead tattoo on the arm has crossed our minds, but it wouldn't do this seagoing rainbow justice.

Steelhead are a separate theology in and of themselves. Deliberating on this sea-run rainbow is enough to get any fervent worshipper up in the freezing predawn, happy at the prospect of wading into bitter-cold water, day in and day out for one fish. Risking marital bliss and courting certain financial ruin, any excuse is a good excuse to cast for steelhead.

Steelhead are sea-run rainbow trout, and they get big. The biggest free-line fish is in the forty-pound range. Unconfirmed, but reputable,

A boil of herring on the water signals actively feeding salmon. Drag your lure around the perimeter.

*Addicted members of the steelhead cult enjoy fast
action on an unusually warm afternoon.*

sources say that a few fish might even make it into the fifties. Still, a five-pounder on the end of any line has a life of its own and lifts your spirits. A ten-pounder makes you feel like you're something special. A fifteen-pounder makes you feel like you're God's gift to the angling world. A twenty-pounder makes you humble.

This fish can spawn several times (unlike salmon, which die after spawning). Depending on its genetic coding, a steelhead will spawn at different times of the year. A winter fish will make its way up the water for the winter run; a fall or summer fish will make its way during the fall or summer. Many steelhead runs, like the runs on Michael's home river, the Rogue, are fairly well delineated.

When a seagoing steelhead hits fresh water, it knows exactly where to go. Male steelhead are usually the first to arrive upriver, making the place nice and cozy for the females that will be coming later. Spawning beds get a lot of use and are returned to year after year.

The female will lay eggs on the gravel bed, a plate-sized hollow scooped about eight inches deep by tail fanning. The water will be from one to five feet deep with good oxygenation. Males fight one another for the right to fertilize the eggs. The hen will lay her eggs, then go upstream a ways and scoop another indentation and spawn again. She'll repeat this process until she's spawned out.

With luck, some of the fry will battle out of the gravel spawning beds, avoid getting eaten, and grow up. From one to four years later, the fish that survive in the ocean will make their way back up the river to spawn in the same area they were born. After spawning, steelhead who survive propagating will rest a bit and drift off down to the ocean to feed and build all the energy they've lost trying to reproduce. If they're lucky they will return and spawn again. Some fish might lose from 35 to 40 percent of their body weight during this process. As a rule, the males get battered pretty bad during the spawn. More females survive than males.

GEARING UP FOR BATTLE

To battle powerful fish like salmon and steelhead you need specialized gear. On the Rogue River one spring, we were fishing with master river guide Jim Dunlevy. We watched a friend, whose name we won't mention, pitch a temper tantrum and nearly start to cry salmon tears. Of course, you'd have cried too. Our friend was one of those sorts who used ultralight gear on everything—against Jim's and our advice. Ultralight gear is fun, but it has a time and a place. Really light rigs on lakers— big fish you can be sure—is one thing. On a river you have current and structure to take into account.

Anyway, he caught a small fish and was smug about his light gear. Later, he fished a good pocket of water not far from the Gold Hill Bridge. Then he got a strike. He set the hook on a really good fish.

Mr. Salmon, who knew it was his lucky day, headed to heavy water. Our friend couldn't turn his fish—a fish that had come out of the water a few times to show us how big he was. Ultralight stuff just wasn't doing the trick. In the first place, the drag on the light reel had just about burned out. The line was too light, and there wasn't enough power in the rod to work the fish. This was a fish of a lifetime, and he lost it.

We're not saying that if our good friend had had the right setup, he would have landed his fish. This is fishing, after all, and there are no guarantees. But he would have had a much better chance with the right gear. As it was, he had no chance at all. For pan-size trout, he was properly rigged. When you factor in a big fish, you have a caster courting disaster.

The Rod. Unless you're after really big Tyee, you can probably use the same rod for both salmon and steelhead. Obviously, if you fish for more steelhead than salmon, go with a light rod. If you fish for more salmon than steelhead, go heavier. Situations vary, but these guidelines will give you an idea.

Steelhead on light tackle are the ultimate challenge, but don't be disappointed if you lose one or two!

Most rods will be from eight to nine feet—giving you the turning torque, the casting power, the hook setting backbone, and the shock absorption you need for powerful fish. If you have to err, err closer to nine feet than eight.

- If you mainly drift-fish, use a moderate-action rod.

- If you fish plugs, use a fast-action rod.

- If you cast a lot, use a fast- or very-fast-action rod that will hold up (like the Sage 570).

- If you spin, use a moderate- to fast-action rod.

The Reel. You need a good reel with a good drag that can take a lot of strain. It must also have adequate line capacity so you won't get spooled when the fish runs (before you can turn it). These powerful fish may actually make several hard runs before tiring. You have to have enough line to check the run. If you'll be casting a lot, a reel that has a smooth retrieve is a good idea. And it doesn't hurt to have a few extra spools filled with line. You wouldn't be the first person to get spooled and lose all your line when a fish ran. Jim Dunlevy uses a reel with 100- to 140-yard spool for steelhead and 150- to 200-yard spool for salmon.

Jim Rough, our good friend and outfitter at Black Gold Lodge in British Columbia, outfits his customers with a mooching rod and reel for ocean-run salmon. Mooching is a slow-water troll using a heavy ball weight as a sort of downrigger. The tackle is similar in design to a fly reel but has a much stiffer drag for open water. Jim likes to drag cut-plug herring soaked in brine, which spins in the water like a top and flashes like a beacon—it drives the big chinook crazy.

When you're trolling (mooching) in the open water and a brute takes your lure, the first thing he'll do is take off like a salmon out of hell, stripping away many a football field of line. The mooching outfit gives him room to run, which is the best way to deal with a strong

A typical day of salmon or steelhead fishing in the Pacific Northwest.

chinook. The fight becomes a great game of give-and-take, and frankly it's a fun way to work the hardware.

The Lines. You need to have a good quality line. This sort of fishing puts a lot of strain on your string. If you're on a budget, you'll need several spools for your single reel, so you can switch lines for different conditions or types of fish.

Some anglers use a much heavier line for salmon and steelhead than for other fish. Consider the average weight of the fish and the water conditions. If you are after chinook, you'll want to go with heavier line. If you are fishing in heavy current and water with a lot of structure, a heavier line makes sense.

For steelhead, the average line is 6- to 15-pound-test. We are especially fond of 8- to 12-pound Stren MagnaThin line. This line has a small diameter so it casts well. It's also very strong. You can get a 12-pound-test line with the average diameter of an 8-pound-test line.

For salmon, the average line is 10- to 35-pound test. For big Alaskan kings that get well over fifty pounds, you'll want heavier lines

WORKING THE WATER CAREFULLY WITH A PLANNED SERIES OF CASTS

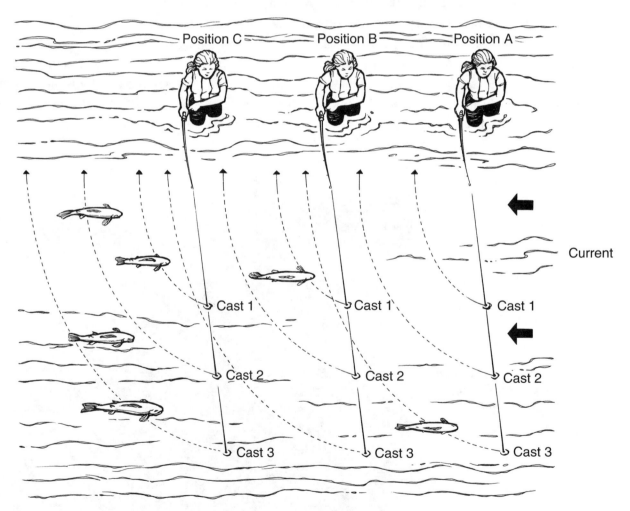

To get more depth from your spinner in fast current, cast upstream, let your lure sink, then retrieve. Work a small section of water, and then move a few feet. Continue this until you have worked all the good water.

upwards of 20-pound-test. For Salmon in Oregon and Washington, we frequently use 12- to 16-pound-test line.

STRATEGIES

Do steelhead eat when they spawn? No. Neither do salmon. (Well, maybe a little when they first enter freshwater and they are still a little salty.) This is an advantage because you don't have to worry about imitating a food source.

As a fish starts toward its journey, certain physiological changes start to take place—a desire to eat is one of the first things to go. As the final destination gets closer, breeding looms and a fish lives off its bodily stores of fat. While the feeding urge shuts down, salmon and steelhead still act out feeding responses.

While they don't eat per se, they will take certain lures right by their mouths out of reflex or habit. Because of the many physiological changes in spawners, some experts feel steelhead might be resorting to early pre-ocean feeding responses when they go for a lure. Maybe it thinks and feeds like it did when it was a young river fish. Or perhaps the spinner is an annoyance or the fish is acting out aggressive behavior.

For those of us who like to catch fish, it's a good thing salmon and steelhead act this way. What the caster tries to do is come up with the right lure action and color to trigger a response. We don't care if it's anger, aggression, annoyance, or an old feeding pattern just as long as the fish strikes our lure when it spins by.

Know When They Run. The first thing you have to do is find out if the fish are running. You need up-to-date information. You can get a pretty good idea, or at least a general idea, by looking in books and magazines. In many areas, the runs are very predictable. Be a detective. Call guides, tackle stores, bait shops, sporting good stores, and the local game and fish office for the hottest information.

Where to Fish. There's a lot of river, and most of it won't have fish in it. You need to look for two things: the migrating paths the fish take up the river and where they rest. You can catch fish in the migratory paths, but you are better off focusing your efforts where the fish rest.

QUARTERING CAST

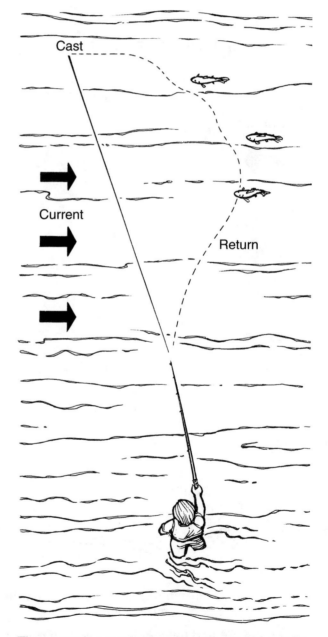

The quartering cast is a good way to provoke a strike from salmon and steelhead. Cast up and across, and bring the lure in across the current.

When you look at the water, look for the easiest access up the stream. The migrating fish will take the course of least resistance to conserve their energy. Fish aren't stupid. It may not seem like it to us, but there are "watery" roads spawning fish travel. Every so often, as you'd expect, the fish needs to rest or hold. Fish rest in water that taxes them least. This is where you want to focus your fishing efforts. A group of fish might hold over for a day or so, a few hours, or just a few minutes. Good resting water is *always* good resting water. If it holds one group of fish now, it will hold others later.

For this reason, many good holding waters are charted and a matter of record, and it's sometimes a race for anglers to stake out a claim on a favorite spot. The caster who gets there first gets the best fishing. A little research will give you a good idea where you should start. Then work the water carefully with a planned

DOWNSTREAM SWING QUARTERING CAST

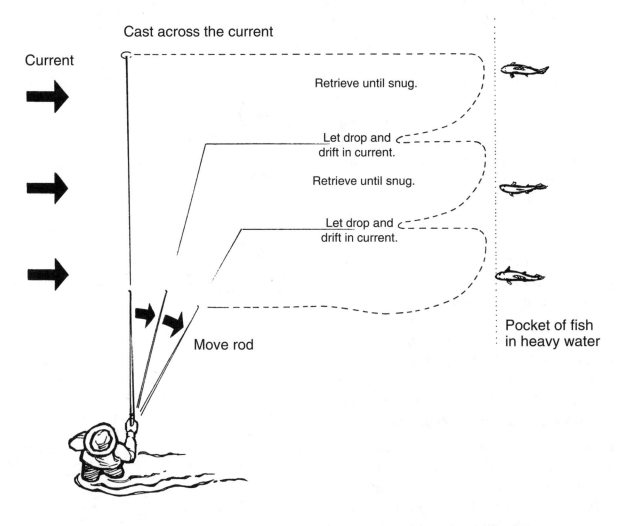

- The downstream swing quartering cast helps you present your lure to a fish as you work the pocket systematically.

- Cast out and let your line drop as it drifts with the current. Then retrieve until you feel the lure. Let it drift and drop. In the meantime, work across the pocket by moving your rod downstream. Let your lure drift; then retrieve.

Alan's addiction to salmon came relatively late in life, but he got hooked after boating his first Tyee. (His wife has never forgiven Michael.)

series of casts. Cast systematically through a small section of water, and then move a few feet and repeat.

A quartering cast effectively works the water to reveal where the fish are holding. Cast upstream and across the current; then bring the lure in across the current to provoke a strike. A downstream swing quartering cast allows you to fish water across the current and downstream from you. It employs a drift, drop, and pulse action that can trigger a salmon or steelhead to respond.

It's often hard to feel the pickup since river-run salmon and steelhead are light biters. Don't get anxious. Wait until you feel the pull before you set the hook. You should also watch for a slack-line pickup, which means the fish has taken the lure and is swimming right toward the boat. If this happens, the best thing you can do is turn the boat and reel fast. Make sure you sharpen your hooks since you'll work dang hard for a single strike. It would be a shame to miss a fish because of a dull hook.

Play the fish. When you do hook a monster, don't be in too big a hurry to get the fish into your net. It really doesn't want to be there, and it'll do everything in its power to stay far from it. Play the fish. Let it get a little winded before you try landing it. On the one hand, enjoy the fight; don't try to make it end too quickly. On the other hand, don't overplay a tired fish either. When the flesh around the hook gets pulled for too long, it expands and you start losing trophies.

16
OTHER FISH WORTH CATCHING
Walleye, Grayling, Panfish, and Whitefish

The world doesn't completely revolve around trout, bass, and salmon. There are a lot of other wonderful fish to catch. Each fish has a few special quirks that set it apart from the others. But fish are fish. They share a number of common denominators. What you learn about one fish will help you hook another.

Let's take a look at a few of our favorite *other* fish.

WALLEYE (*STIZOSTEDION VITREUM VITREUM*)

There's a cult following this fish—a group of bug-eyed walleye-infatuated casters who would rather cast to walleye than have true love. These folks aren't quite as crazy as the steelhead cult, but they aren't far behind.

Walleye roam, eating anything in their way. With this proclivity for wandering, one of the

Elitists may scoff, but who can argue with a catch like this?

challenges is finding them. Walleye like to school up, and where you catch one you'll often catch others, mostly the same size.

The walleye is an olive brown fish with a dark back and head and creamy yellow lower sides and belly. Some grow very large, and people have caught walleye in the twenty-plus-pound range. Most of us, however, will never see a fish that size.

In the olden days, walleye swam the central and northeastern waters of the United States and Canada. However, this fish has been successfully transplanted to a number of waters far from its ancestral home. Careless "dumping" of walleye has ruined many good trout lakes because trout can't compete with them.

Even though walleye can be hard to find at times, they prefer gravelly, sandy, or rocky bottoms in cold, clean water. They prefer water temperatures in the high 50s to middle 60s. During the day, they take shelter in deeper water—especially if the water is warm or the day is hot. When the water is cooler, and during fall and spring, walleye hold closer to shore. During the warmer months, fish will work closer to shore in the evening and after dark, and at this time fishing can be excellent.

Walleye spawn in the spring sometime after the ice melts and the water temperature reaches between 39 and 45 degrees. Fish will either swim upstream or congregate near rocky shoals. Males come first, followed by the females. The average fish remains in the spawning area from four to six weeks. During this time, they are very aggressive and will hit anything that flutters by them. In the West, where

Walleye can be great little fighters; fun, and somewhat eerie, fish to pursue.

walleye fishing is more difficult, the spawn is a great time to nail a few fish. After spawning they don't stick around to watch over the young.

GRAYLING (*THYMALLUS ARCTICUS*)

An adult grayling is one of the most handsome fish swimming—as lovely as the sky-blue waters it calls home. If you ever have the privilege of catching one, take a long look at *Thymallus,* and then look again. The purplish hues of color seem to shift in the light.

The sail-like dorsal fin (more than seventeen rays, in case you are interested) that sometimes extends to the adipose fin on males is the grayling's most prominent feature. Purple hues from the cheek to the tail are accented by stripes and a few wonderful spots. The body, depending on the water and other conditions, is a shiny, khaki green but can range from silver to light bronze.

Izaak Walton suggests in *The Compleat Angler* that a grayling has "a tender mouth and he's oftener lost" once a caster has hooked him. The notion that the fish is hard to hold has lingered for centuries, but there's nothing tender about this fish's mouth. Rather, the grayling has a small mouth and the clever angler will use a small lure when casting for this pure-water trophy. European anglers revere the grayling, which has an equal status with the trout. In continental folklore, the grayling often feeds on small pieces of gold and its flesh (especially its fat) can help fight illnesses.

A record grayling would be a fish in the five-plus pound range. Fish of this size come from the high north. An angler once caught a fish just shy of six pounds in the Northwest Territories. The longest fish taken was just under twenty-two inches. For most of us common folk, however, any fish that is near two pounds is really fine—especially in the lower forty-eight. A fish in the three-pound class is a really good fish in northern Canada or Alaska.

Grayling fishing is some of the finest you'll have, not only because grayling are excellent trophies, but because they are blessed to live in some of the finest real estate God made. The

Grayling are easily identifiable by their floppy, extra-large dorsal fin, which never fails to delight anglers.

grayling lives only in the coldest, purest waters, and its ideal temperature range is between 47 and 52 degrees. Many of the waters it haunts are ice-capped over eight months of the year. The water in these areas is rather low in oxygen, and other game fish such as trout would find survival tough.

The grayling is an environmental barometer that we need to watch more carefully. The Michigan species was so plentiful it was sold commercially at fish markets in Chicago and Detroit. Fish were hauled out by the wagon load—in the 1870s no one thought its numbers would ever be depleted. Due to logging pressures (which raised hell with the watersheds and water temperature) and overfishing, by 1880 this subspecies had nearly gone the way of the passenger pigeon. Nearly overnight it was gone.

This fish simply won't tolerate any impurity or warming of the water system. The fish is equally at home in lakes or rivers. Canada and Alaska are the largest untracked grayling waters on this continent. However, waters in Montana, Washington, Wyoming, Colorado, Idaho, and Utah support good populations.

It's our opinion that Wyoming has the best grayling water outside Canada and Alaska. Meadow Lake at the foot of the Wind River Mountain Range holds some of the largest fish we've seen in the two-and-a-half-pound range.

Depending on the water temperature and other factors, a hen will produce about twelve thousand eggs sometime between March and early June. To deposit her eggs, a female grayling will find shallow and fast-moving feeder streams. A male will establish its territory and defend it from other fish—using his big fin as a shield.

Grayling school, so the trick is often locating the fish. In a river they are likely to suspend in pools and riffles. However, we suggest you start fishing the deepest holes and pockets first, especially if they are choked with structure that break up the current.

On lakes, look for points, coves, or structure first. Look for rising fish. Work the shoreline casually until you start picking up strikes—then work the area more carefully. Be aware that at certain times, fish hold near the bottom and you'll need to get your lure down to them.

The best fishing for grayling is early morning and late evening; however, you can catch them at any time of the day.

There's nothing lukewarm about this fish. When it's feeding it will take just about anything you throw at it. The grayling isn't aware that something in its universe is out to trick it. In this fish's world, if it looks like food, it must be food. When grayling are on the prowl, you'll catch a lot of them.

PANFISH YOU HAVE TO LOVE

Most of the time, panfish don't grow huge, but they're fun to hook and fun to eat. Because panfish tend to stunt, keeping a mess of them for the skillet is healthy for the population. We both aren't much for fried food, but there's nothing like a bluegill, perch, or crappie battered up and fried. Makes you hungry just thinking about it.

These little suckers breed fast, even if they don't get really big. These are fish for your ultralight tackle. These are also wonderful fish to start your kids on—only watch out for the sharp spines. Light line and light tackle make these fish more of a challenge and a blast to hook. Basically $\frac{1}{4}$- to $\frac{1}{32}$-ounce spinners and jigs will cover most situations.

Panfish can be finicky. You'll have to work with your retrieve. Sometimes a fast retrieve will draw a strike; other times, they want a slow retrieve. You'll also need to experiment with water depth. You can cast all day with nothing to show for it if you don't play with depths. Depending on the water temperature and time of the year, these little fish might be deep or

A FISH FINDER EXHIBITS HIS GOODS.

shallow. Once you find where fish are, you'll obviously want to stay there.

While these little finned foes aren't big, they are vicious predators in their own right. They attack without quarter. Look for them around old logs, wrecked cars, docks, weed lines, and shelves.

Bluegill
(Lepomis machrochirus)

A bluegill is a sunfish (sometimes called bream or brim) and is probably the most popular panfish, likely one of the first fish many of us hooked into. While they are usually pretty easy to catch, sometimes this little devil can shut the best of us down. Still, they keep you coming back.

The bluegill is bluish green accented with orange and red on its lower parts. The back of the fish is darkest, the sides being lighter. Many fish have dark bars on the sides.

Any fish over a foot is a dang good fish. Some fish have reached fifteen to sixteen inches, but these individuals are somewhat rare. The largest fish might hit four pounds. Some of the fish we've caught have been in the one-pound range—but we've caught literally bucket loads that were one-half to three-quarters of a pound.

Originally, the bluegill ranged from southeastern Canada to Georgia and Texas. In the 1800s the fish was transplanted to the West Coast. Nowadays, you can find them most anywhere. The fish is highly adaptable and is a favorite stock fish for private ponds.

Bluegills like calm water with lots of plant life. Plant life is critical since it's a bluegills feeding ground, rich with insects and other aquatic life, and a good hiding place. Bluegills aren't very high on the food chain. Big fish get fat munching down our bluish little friend.

They can be moody, but some of the really great fishing occurs when the water reaches the high 60s and low 70s. The best time to fish is morning and evening. During the day, bigger 'gills hold in deeper water, coming into the shallows to feed when the light is lower.

You can fish for them fine from shore. These fish will take almost anything you throw at them—as long as it's small (their mouths aren't big, obviously). During the day, the smaller fish will hold by structure near the shore. The bigger fish will stay in the deeper water and come in closer to shore during the evening and morning.

Depending on the water and the part of the country, bluegills spawn from spring to mid-summer when the water temperature approaches 70 degrees (in some areas, even higher). If the conditions are right, this little sunfish will keep spawning all summer long.

These little fighters are rather liberated. The males build the nests in shallow water, about two to three feet deep, over gravel or sandy bottoms. The nests look like mashed potatoes before you put the gravy on. Often, where you'll find one, you'll find others—they like to stick together. They are very protective if something, such as your lure, comes in toward the nest.

Yellow Perch
(*Perca flavescens*)

For many anglers, the yellow perch may be the first fish they ever caught. Called the yellow perch, the ringed perch, or the American perch, this is one of the most dispersed fish in this country and one of the most beloved warm-water game fishes. The fish gets a real foothold in some waters, where it becomes less

beloved by serious trout anglers who see their water choked out by this fish. While perch do not get very big, they are very good eating—always take a limit home (they tend to overpopulate, which stunts their size).

A fish that reaches two pounds would be a very large specimen, although a few have been nailed at about five pounds. Because of stunting, the average fish most anglers catch is about a half pound. The perch isn't a fast growing fish; thus, it's good forage for hungry neighbors.

Perch spawn in the spring. When the water temperature reaches between 45 and 51 degrees, the hen lays her eggs. The sticky eggs are laid in long, flat lines over vegetation. Fry hatch in about ten days.

The kids in our neighborhood spend hours dropping a line for these fish, which are fairly easy to catch. The action can often be rapid (the fish travel in schools), and they taste good. This hearty little fish doesn't put up much of a fight but will take about anything you throw at him. Small spinners such as Panther Martins, Jake's Spinners, and Super Dupers work the best. Fishing is usually best from early afternoon to evening. Start by working your lure or jig about ten to twenty inches off the bottom.

Black Crappie
(*Pomoxis nigomaculatus*)

Folks fish for the crappie because they're abundant, easy to catch, and fight hard. (For the record, there is also a white crappie, which is similar.) This fish originally called southern Canada home. Thanks to transplanting, it's all over in some degree or another.

The black crappie is olive with a lot of blackish green blotches on the sides and top, but color varies depending on the water and temperature. The average fish is from eleven to thirteen inches. In the most ideal waters, some have pushed five pounds.

Great fishing begins in the spring before the spawn occurs. Crappies spawn in late May and early June, when the water gets between 58 and 64 degrees. The males fan out bowls on the muddy bottom—in about six to eight feet of water—to guard the nest. At this time, they become extremely protective of their nest and will aggressively strike a lure fished over their bed.

Crappies hold in pretty large schools. Once you find where they are, the action is fast and furious. Fish small spinners (Panther Martin, Super Duper #503, Rooster Tail) just off the bottom, or work a minnow imitation, with or without a spinner, at varying speeds.

MOUNTAIN WHITEFISH (*PROSOPIUM WILLIAMSONI*)

Whitefish don't get much respect. It's too bad that many fisherman consider them trash, because they seem to be active when trout aren't feeding and are a great way to break the winter doldrums.

If you're fishing for trout, sooner or later you're going to latch into a whitefish by accident. They don't get very big—a three pounder is a good-size fish. The state record in Utah is four pounds seven ounces. As the name implies, they are white to light brown with silver sides. The face and lower jaw are blunt. The mouth looks a little like a sucker's.

You'll generally catch whitefish on wet flies and very small lures—Panther Martins are good to start with. You'll also catch more in the fall and winter than at any other time of the year. They seem to thrive on cold water and fight twice as hard as trout in the winter.

Because whitefish eat the same food as trout, we fish similar lures for both. A #16 or #18 Pheasant Tail, Hare's Ear, or Chamois Nymph fished with a light leader (3-pound-test) is very effective. I've also taken a few on Glo Bugs during the trout spawn. Many whitefish experts like dark spinners and flies,

Michael netted this whitefish back in his long-haired prime and celebrated the catch by smashing his rod Jimi Hendrix style.

but we've had good luck with flies tied with reds and pinks.

Whitefish are a little bony unless filleted, but they are very tasty fried. Most of the time whitefish are smoked. The flesh is a little oily, which makes them perfect for the smoker. In nearly all waters that we know of, taking a large batch from the stream (usually the limit is two or three times the limit for trout) won't hurt the population at all.

Look for whites to congregate at the bottom of riffles in the tail of a pool. Shotgun the riffles—work all the water with your lure or fly. They sometimes move into these waters to feed. Remember their mouths are very, very small. You need to use the smallest spinners you can find ($\frac{1}{32}$ ounce to start with). Go heavier since these fish, as a general rule, hug the bottoms.

17
BUMP-AND-TICKLE JIGGING
Getting the Big Mack to Attack

Certainly deep-water jigging for lake trout or mackinaws isn't new. Traditionally, jigs and spoons have been fished through the ice, right after ice-off, and in the fall. Large jigs and spoons have been the lures of choice for decades. But, for many anglers, jigging has been a hit-and-miss affair. If you're lucky enough to get into aggressive fish, you're going to get pickups and have the ride of your life. But it's a random act of fishing faith. There is little craft to it. An angler simply drops his line and jigs. Our friend Steve Partridge has made it an art

form and a serious way to catch fish for the serious angler.

Thus, bump and tickle comes into play. Yes, the bump and tickle. It sounds a little lewd at first, but what's obscene is how it attracts big fish. The nice thing is this method will work on any mack water. In fact, it will work on any game fish. When you bump and tickle, you use as small a jig as you can get away with and still feel the bottom. Determine the size by the depth or the surface water conditions. Certainly, this method triggers aggressive fish. More important,

This fine mackinaw, hooked by Michael, is what bump-and-tickle fishing is all about.

it works well on neutral fish that will often ignore a big lure or one that jumps abruptly. A big lure may even spook a fish. A smaller jig, worked properly, though, will often provoke a response, and your arm will be a lot less sore at the end of the day.

pensive rods and reels; lead core, steel, or copper line; and a thousand expensive lures. All that's needed is a good stiff rod, a reel with good line capacity, and a selection of jigs.

The Rod. Start with a rod that is stiff but sensitive. (We like the Team Diawa Tournament

WATER CONDITIONS			
FEET OF WATER	ROUGH, BUT FISHABLE	CALM, BUT RIFFLED	FLAT, NO RIFFLE
25 to 50	¾-oz. lure	½-oz. lure	¼-oz. lure
75	1- to 2-oz. lure	¾-oz. lure	¼- to ½-oz. lure
100	1- to 2-oz. lure	¾- to 1½-oz. lure	½- to 1-oz. lure

- When the water is flat, you can use a smaller jig or lure. When the wind starts to pick up and the boat starts to drift—often with the afternoon breeze—you need to increase the weight of your jig or lure so you can contact the bottom. Try ³⁄₈- to ¹⁄₂-ounce jigs in calm water and ³⁄₄- to 2-ounce jigs in deep water and windy conditions.

- At first you might want to use the same size jig all the time so you get a good feel for the weight of the lure. Remember, any deviation in the feel, any at all, could be a fish.

- Some casters wrap their index finger with a wrap of line. You feel the fish with your finger before you feel it with your rod tip.

- If you have an electronic trolling motor, you can keep positioning your boat so you keep your line vertical—90 degrees to the surface. Note any twitches signaling a strike.

- If you don't keep your line taunt or if there are any bows in the line, you'll miss subtle pickups.

This means the average fisherman can catch good-size mack, sometimes even trophy-size fish, without shark tackle and all that fancy down rigging. There is no need for heavy, ex-

Series 5′9″ Finesse spinning rods and the 6′3″ Twitchin' rod). Use line as light as you feel comfortable with. Lighter line makes it easier to feel the lure.

Nearly all mackinaw fishing is done in deeper water, from fifty to a hundred feet. Except when very aggressive, lakers hold on the bottom, which is where your lure has to be. Feel is the key. If you lose bottom, you've lost control and you're jigging blindly. Most successful fishing in deep water will be less than three to four feet off the bottom. If a fisherman has control, he can discreetly work his lure and give a neutral fish time to investigate— and realize how hungry it is. Also, the nonaggressive fish won't be spooked by the small, dancing motions. He may even be stimulated to strike.

The Reel. You'll need a good reel with a large line capacity. A good-size mack can sound from here to Atlantis, stripping off plenty of mono as he goes.

You also need a good, consistent drag that won't burn up after a few fish. Big lakers put a lot of pressure on equipment. You fish long and hard for every bite. It's a tragedy to lose one because of equipment failure.

Our friend and guide Steve Partridge holds a nice fish before releasing it.

The Jigs. Some mack anglers always stay with heavier jigs and spoons because they are easier to keep in contact with the bottom. A smaller jig takes a little more practice and a lot more concentration, but it's not hard to learn how to use. The trick is always feeling the jig so you can do what Steve calls "controlling the bottom." This means you always know where your jig is in relation to the bottom.

It seems like a leap of faith, but diminutive action has better net results than the opposite. To convince yourself, watch your jig in a foot of water. Notice how your jig dances with even the slightest twitch. You usually don't come across an aggressive fish in deep water. You'll entice more action with subtle movements.

Another way to improve your learning curve in deep water is to watch your jig on the fish finder. You'll be quite pleased with the number of big fish that come over to investigate. If you're still not sure, try some radical jigging when a big lunker swims in for a look. More often than not, you will spook it.

The first problem is getting the fish to the jig. Even a laker's vision is somewhat inhib-ited in deep water, so you need to try and stimulate some of the fish's other senses. The *bump* of bump and tickle is the first step in trying to get a fish interested. The bump or thud the lure makes when it hits the bottom causes a vibration that is picked up by the fish's lateral line,

Jigging is not only a great way to catch lakers, it's also an effective way to catch any game fish. Here is a nice cutthroat caught by jigging off the bottom of Strawberry Reservoir.

BUMP-AND-TICKLE TECHNIQUES

BASIC BUMP-AND-TICKLE PATTERN #1

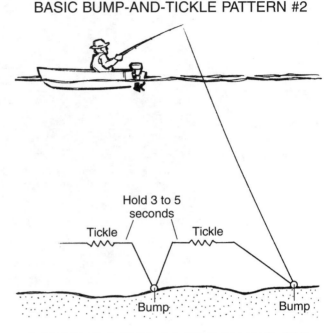

Let jig or lure hit bottom, lift 6 inches, hold for 3 seconds, tickle 3 to 5 seconds, hold 3 seconds, bump, repeat.

BASIC BUMP-AND-TICKLE PATTERN #2

Let jig hit bottom, lift 3 feet, hold 3 to 5 seconds, tickle, hold, tickle, bump, repeat.

BASIC BUMP-AND-TICKLE PATTERN #3

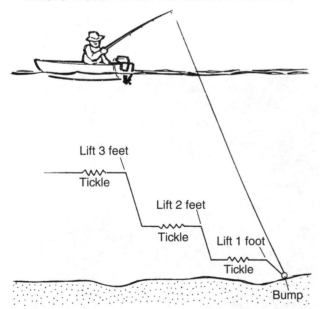

Let jig hit bottom, lift 1 foot, hold for 3 to 5 seconds, tickle and hold twice. Lift 2 feet, tickle, hold twice, then lift to 3 feet, bump, repeat.

BASIC BUMP-AND-TICKLE PATTERN #4

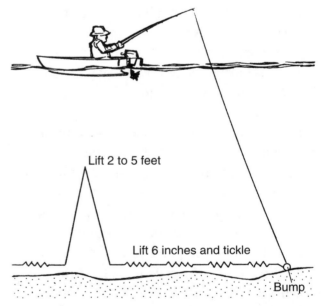

Let jig hit bottom, lift 1 to 6 inches, do a series of hold and tickle. Lift jig 2 to 5 feet, drop to same depth, do a series of hold and tickle, repeat.

Michael's friend Lee Nelson holds a lake trout he nailed in one hundred feet of water. Catching a fish like this is a great thrill.

a series of nerve endings along the length of the fish. Remember, a fish can hear a lot farther than it can see. And while the lure's movement in the water also sends a signal, the fish can't pick up such vibrations as far away. The bump signals the fish to come over and investigate, even if it's not hungry. In effect, you're increasing your fishing area considerably.

The bump or vibration is your first attractor. Many anglers just jig, but here you are actively trying to hit the bottom—and will do it again and again as you work the water.

After feeling the jig hit the bottom, carefully pick it up two inches to a foot. Then, "tickle" the jig up and down for three or four seconds with one- to two-inch strokes. Use only enough movement necessary to get the tail to undulate.

Work the tickle motion again, or drop the lure for another bump. After the tickle, it's important to let the lure stand still for several seconds. This is often when the fish strikes. Most anglers get impatient and don't let the lure sit after they've moved it. It's uncomfortable at first, but it works. Waiting drove Alan nuts. But after watching Steve land a couple of forty-pounders in one morning, Alan got with his program.

This is the basic bump-and-tickle form. You can also follow other patterns for the tickle or add a lift. It's hard to believe a jig so delicately moved can produce fish. Since we were so used to radical jigging, Steve suggested we follow a pattern, at least at first, to keep our motions more delicate. A laker can attack at any time, but as most jiggers know, many bite when the jig is still or falling. During the free fall, it's critical to watch your line and rod tip carefully. Set the hook if there's even the slightest hesitation because the bite is often soft and delicate.

You can bump and tickle jig anywhere the water is flat enough that you can control the bottom. Most lakes get a wind by the afternoon, often making it difficult to jig effectively. In the afternoon, many experts, Steve being no exception, leave the large bays and look for narrow fingers of deep water. There are plenty of places to spend the afternoon bumping the bottom where the wind and waves won't ruin your game plan. Tight canyon walls, protected from the winds, are made to order. Fish open stretches of water in the early mornings and evenings.

If You Want to Know More

Bass Myths Exploded. Jerry Gibbs. New York: David McKay Company, Inc. 1978. This is a good discussion for serious bass anglers. You'll learn a lot about bass fishing, and it's fun reading. This book is out of print but easy to find in used bookstores.

Camping Made Easy. Michael Rutter. Old Saybrook, Conn.: Globe Pequot Press. 1997. Yes, this is a camping book. However, it contains a very good discussion on fishing with children.

The Compleat Angler. Izaak Walton. New York: Harper Trade. 1997. Written by the great master during the English Renaissance, this charming book is a must-read for anyone who loves fishing, history, or great fishing literature.

Fly Fishing for the Compleat Idiot. Michael Rutter. Missoula, Mont.: Mountain Press. 1995. While written to the fly caster, this book offers outstanding discussions about specific fish and about reading the water.

Fly Fishing Made Easy. Michael Rutter. Old Saybrook, Conn.: Globe Pequot Press. 1997. The discussion in this book on individual fish species will be very helpful to the budding spin caster.

Freshwater Wilderness: Yellowstone Fishes and Their World. John D. Varley and Paul Schullery. Yellowstone National Park: The Yellowstone Library and Museum Association. 1983. A great semitechnical book about the Yellowstone ecosystem and its fish. This text is well illustrated and carefully put together. It has good general fish information.

The Illustrated Encyclopedia of Fly Casting. New York: Henry Holt. 1993. This book is geared to fly casters, but it contains abundant information about fishing in general. This excellent reference will be a welcome addition to your library.

Lefty's Little Tips. Lefty Kreh. Birmingham, Ala.: Odysseus Editions. 1991. There are a lot of very handy tips that will help the spin caster improve his or her game. This handy little reference is also fun to read.

McClane's New Standard Fishing Encyclopedia, edited by A. J. McClane. New York: Random House. 1998. If you are only going to have one reference book, this one, while expensive and very thick, is a worthwhile investment. It's the best general reference ever written.

Selective Trout. Doug Swisher. New York: Lyons Press. 1983. Here's another book geared to fly casting but with a lot of general information about picky fish and reading the water that will be of value to any caster.

Sierra Trout Guide. Ralf Cutter. Portland, Ore.: Frank Amato Publications. 1991. This book is written for Sierra anglers, but the material on trout, especially native trout, is excellent. The discussions are clear, easy to follow, and fact packed. It will help a trout angler on any water.

Spinning for Trout. Bob Gooch. New York: Scribners. 1981. This book is rather outdated and may only be found in a library or used bookstore. Nevertheless, it is a good reference—and a discussion of fishing the way it used to be. This book at one time was the spin caster's bible.

Spoon Plugging. E. L. "Buck" Perry. Buck Perry Publications. 1979. Buck is no writer, but he is one of the greatest fishermen we've ever met. This book is packed with useful information—especially helpful for the bass and warm-water caster. Buck's method of spoon jigging is very useful. It's the best discussion on structure we've seen. It will help you catch fish. Pike fishermen: read this!

Trout Country. Michael Furtman. Minocqua, Wisc.: NorthWood Press, Inc. 1995. This book holds a wealth of information, and the photographs and illustrations are wonderful. Though very expensive, it's a nice one to have in your library. It is a great treatise on the cycle of life in a trout stream and the life cycle of the trout.

The Ways of the Trout. Leonard Wright. New York: Lyons Press. 1985. A pretty good book that could benefit from better graphics—but it treats the story of wild trout very well. It's packed with little-known tidbits. An enjoyable, informative read.

Whirling Disease Foundation. You can find information online about whirling disease at www.whirling-disease.org.

Michael Rutter with a spring steelhead on the Rogue River

J. Alan Baumgarten with a late-autumn brown trout on the Provo River

ABOUT THE AUTHORS

Michael Rutter and **J. Alan Baumgarten** wrote this book from their fishing experience—they're on the water about a hundred days a year. The award-winning author of *Fly Fishing for the Compleat Idiot* (0-87842-313-3), Rutter has written thirty-seven books, as well as hundreds of articles for magazines like *Outdoor Life* and *Sports Afield*. He teaches English at Brigham Young University when he isn't fishing. Baumgarten is a consultant and editor for outdoor and educational publications, a newspaper columnist and humorist, a Web site developer, and the author or coauthor of twelve books. Both of these fishing fanatics live along the Wasatch Front in Utah.

ABOUT THE ILLUSTRATORS

E. R. Jenne, a professional illustrator for more than twenty years, likes to draw almost as much as he likes to fish. He lives in Missoula, Montana.

Greg Siple is art director for Adventure Cycling Association in Missoula, Montana. Although more a bicyclist than an angler, he did fish off a dock in Florida once in the 1950s.

INDEX

Check for Mountain Press books at your local bookstore. Most stores will be happy to order any titles they do not stock. You may also order directly from us, either with the enclosed order form, by calling our toll-free number (800-234-5308) using your MasterCard or Visa, or via our website: www.montana.com/mtnpress. We will gladly send you a free catalog upon request.

Some other outdoor titles of interest:

_____*Fly Fishing for the Compleat Idiot*	$15.00
_____*Fly Tying: Adventures in Fur, Feathers, and Fun*	$18.00
_____*The Montanans' Fishing Guide West*	$18.00
_____*Packin' In on Mules and Horses*	$18.00

Please include $3.00 per order to cover shipping and handling.

Send the books marked above. I have enclosed $_____

Name_____

Address_____

City_____State_____Zip_____

☐ Payment enclosed (check or money order in U.S. funds)

Bill my: ☐ VISA ☐ MasterCard   Expiration Date:_____

Card No._____

Signature _____

MOUNTAIN PRESS PUBLISHING COMPANY
1301 S. Third St. W. • P.O. Box 2399 • Missoula, Montana 59806
e-mail: mtnpress@montana.com • website: www.mtnpress.com
Order toll-free 1-800-234-5308—have your Visa or MasterCard ready.